contemporary
cross stitch
for soft furnishings

contemporary cross stitch

for soft furnishings

caroline birkett

hamlyn

First published in Great Britain in 2001
by Hamlyn, an imprint of Octopus
Publishing Group Limited
2–4 Heron Quays, London E14 2JP

Text copyright © 2001 Caroline Birkett
Copyright © 2001 Octopus Publishing
Group Limited

Distributed in the United States by
Sterling Publishing Co. Inc.,
387 Park Avenue South, New York, NY
10016-8810

A catalogue record for this book is
available from the British Library

ISBN 0 600 60042 4

Printed in China

introduction 6

the natural room 8

Take your colour cue from nature and
create a peaceful interior. Use fabrics with
a natural texture such as linen, calico and
muslin in uncluttered rooms with elements
of wood, stone, wicker and raffia.

ivy spiral 12

A spiral of ivy winds its way to the centre of a
circular cushion

Skill level **Intermediate**

fossil appliqué 18

Ammonites stitched on frayed squares and
appliquéd on to a square cushion

Skill level **Easy**

sea shells 22

Shells stitched between pleats on palest grey-
blue silk

Skill level **Advanced**

patchwork hellebore 28

Cross stitch combined in a simple machine
patchwork for this green-themed cushion

Skill level **Easy**

the rich room 32

Carved furniture combines with
intensely coloured soft furnishings in
luxurious velvets and silks to create a
warm and seductive interior.

organza leaf 36

A Japanese maple leaf of layered organza
edged with cross stitching

Skill level **Advanced**

chilli peppers 42

Red chilli peppers stitched on to golden-
yellow evenweave fabric and appliquéd
around a scarlet velvet bolster cushion

Skill level **Intermediate**

peacock and jewel 46

The iridescent colours of a peacock
feather stitched with metallic threads on a
fringed cushion

Skill level **Advanced**

gladiolus 50

A single gladiolus sits comfortably
between blocks of gold on this unusual
rectangular cushion

Skill level **Intermediate**

the bright room 54

A dash of colour lightens the mood in a minimal bleached-wood interior – a room flooded with colour is filled with energy and brilliance.

flower power 58
Iris, anemone and helianthus scattered across a cushion of white evenweave linen

Skill level **Intermediate**

tropical knit 62
A knitted cushion with a jacquard stripe design and a cross stitch melon motif

Skill level **Advanced**

citrus 66
Orange, lemon and lime buttons add zest to rectangular cushions in citrus colours

Skill level **Intermediate**

trailing nasturtiums 70
A bright cushion covered with orange nasturtiums climbing through turquoise borders

Skill level **Easy**

the pale room 74

Fresh and clean or faded and worn, pale colours are calming and easy to live with. Combine the watery and chalky colours of laminated furniture with frosted glass or sheer fabrics with colourwashed wood.

modesty 78
Antique white stitches on violet fabric capture the classical beauty of a 17th-century marble bust

Skill level **Intermediate**

heartsease 82
Flowerheads worked on squares of voile for a delicate cushion

Skill level **Intermediate**

feathers 86
Swan feathers in white stitches drift airily across pale blue fabric

Skill level **Intermediate**

clover 92
Clover borders worked down the sides of a rectangular cushion finished with antique lace

Skill level **Easy**

materials, 96 equipment and techniques

introduction

  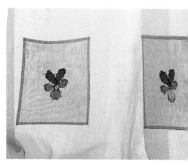

Some of the most welcoming homes are those with real personality – environments that are continually evolving to reflect the new experiences and interests of the people living there. Successful rooms are created by following feelings more than theory and can incorporate a collision of influences, mixing old and new to create a vibrant environment full of contrasts and surprises. Colour can be used to create cohesion, bringing together the different elements of a room in a broad, flexible way.

Each chapter of this book begins with some key ideas for developing the potential of a room, with the aim of strengthening its identity within one of the basic groups of colours – natural, rich, pale and bright. There are four embroidery designs capturing the spirit of each of these palettes, intended initially to be worked as cushions but accompanied by suggestions on how the designs could be used differently on other soft furnishings.

Cushions are both the 'jewellery' of a room and an invaluable aid to relaxation, providing comfort, softness and support. They can be used to mix, contrast or harmonize colours and to introduce texture and pattern. With the array of coloured threads available and the beautiful, precise texture of its stitches, cross stitch can be used to create magical cushions with great impact.

Although less obvious, other soft furnishings become something special when embroidered with a small design detail. No machine can reproduce cross stitching exactly, which gives each piece an individuality. The spirit of the stitcher

comes through in small imperfections, such as a slight variation in the size and tension of the stitches, which simply add to its appeal.

Many people are currently rediscovering the therapeutic value of stitching and the sense of achievement that can be gained from creating an object that is both useful and beautiful. Cross stitch is one of the oldest embroidery stitches and one of the simplest to master. Two straight diagonal stitches form an X, to create a small block of colour, which can be used to construct an immense variety of work, large or small in scale, simple or finely detailed, multicoloured or monochrome.

Cross stitch has a long history and has played an important role in traditions across almost every culture. From its humble beginnings as a means of joining animal skins in ancient times, the technique evolved over many centuries into a decorative and ornamental craft. Cross stitch as we would recognize it today started with the early samplers of the 16th century, featuring bird, flower and house motifs within a border. Functional embroidery of the family initials on clothing and household linens led to decorative embroidery for the home. In the 20th century the craft lost popularity for a while with the advent of mass-produced decorative textiles, but we are now seeing the renaissance of cross stitch.

The projects in this book have been designed with a wide range of styles and colour choices in mind to reflect the variety of inspirations that now influence the decoration of our homes. Cross stitch is a traditional needlecraft, but it is also versatile and is not restricted to any particular style of design. It is a useful, expressive and beautiful medium, perfect for creating contemporary soft furnishings that will also be treasured for generations to come.

the natural room

Whatever the individual style, taking your colour inspiration from nature will create a timeless and versatile interior. Respond to the changing seasons by changing displays and furnishings to create different atmospheres at different times of the year.

Painting walls in muted colours that are barely there creates a neutral shell within which the room can come together. A surprisingly wide choice of shades makes up the neutral palette, from warm, pinky hues to those with a cooler, blue tone. Fresh green-whites tend to be the best choice for sunny rooms, gentler yellowy greens for those that receive sun in the afternoon, and warm pink- or yellow-whites for shady rooms or those that receive sun in the morning. The addition of earthy chocolate-brown and caramel in the soft furnishings will warm and enrich the room in the winter months.

Building textural contrast into the natural room is just as important as choosing and combining colours. Materials can be hard or soft, rough or smooth, shiny or matt, translucent or opaque, regular or random. Although natural colours do not have instant impact, colour in conjunction with

natural

Nature provides a profusion of treasures to collect and display. Stones, shells and coral can be arranged on a plain glass dish or simply mounted in a frame. Fresh flowers and foliage bring nature indoors and with their living power create a calming, therapeutic oasis.

Imaginative texture brings a room to life. A paint on smooth plaster can appear to be a very different colour from the same colour on rough brick because different textures reflect light differently. In the evening artificial light from a number of different sources will more closely reproduce some of the subtlety and variety of natural light. Accent lighting on key features can create added drama by casting interesting shadows, while candles have a meditative quality that brings a space alive with dancing light.

Simple window treatments work well in a natural room. Lightweight fabrics, loosely gathered, can be looped or tied to a pole for an informal appearance. Blinds in linen or raffia create a cleaner line that can be softened with the addition of embroidery or trimmings.

Natural materials age well, making them perfect for flooring, and there are plenty from which to choose. Wood is the most widely used natural flooring and can be treated to alter the colour and finish by waxing, staining or painting. Existing floorboards can be renovated or a new wooden floor laid in strips, blocks or parquet, but nothing could be better in the natural room than floorboards that have mellowed in colour, improving with time and the patina of use. Cork is relatively inexpensive and is hardwearing and cushioning underfoot. Brick and stone are more suited to the hallway, kitchen or dining area as they can be cold. There is now a wide range of natural mattings in seagrass, sisal, coir, jute or rush. Seagrass is smooth, while coir is prickly and jute soft but not very hardwearing, so choose a matting suitable for the location.

For soft furnishings and accessories for the natural room, the emphasis is on simplicity and functionality. Nature lies at the heart of the Japanese aesthetic, and there is much that we can learn from this and use. Great value is placed on the integrity of materials and craftsmanship, while an appreciation of the luxury of space is demonstrated by restraint. When form and function come together perfectly, the status of everyday objects is elevated. Cream or white crockery on an antique linen tablecloth creates a simple but welcoming table. Wicker baskets and linen-covered boxes provide storage that need not be hidden away, and a large wooden bowl containing golden-yellow pears speckled with green is as decorative as any vase of flowers.

Nature provides a profusion of treasures to collect and display. Stones, shells and coral can be arranged on a plain glass dish or simply mounted in a frame. Fresh flowers and foliage bring nature indoors and with their living power create a calming, therapeutic oasis. Flowers that are seasonal and occur in the local climate look and feel most natural. Loose, unstructured displays of fragrant herbs, grasses and leaves have an understated beauty in the variety of their shapes and colours that is sometimes easier to appreciate without the distraction of showy flowers.

Fossils, shells, ivy and the unusual green flower of the hellebore inspired the embroidery designs for the natural room. Piles of plain cushions in contrasting textures, such as raw silk, linen and strokable fur fabrics, provide comfort and warmth. Hand embroidery adds personal detail and individuality to a room with a restful, unchallenging ambience, elevating it from potential blandness. Blankets, throws and informal tie-on covers for chairs in soft, muted tones of luxurious fabrics can all be enhanced with embroidery, creating a special retreat in which to relax and regenerate. The natural room can provide an antidote to the outside world, where the senses are constantly bombarded by noise, pollution and frenetic activity.

ivy spiral

The dark green, heart-shaped leaves of the ivy contrast cleanly with the antique white linen background of this circular cushion. The spiral is a common growth pattern in nature and an appropriate shape with which to emphasize the progressive change in the colour and size of the leaves towards the outer edge of the cushion.

The understated beauty of the common ivy (*Hedera helix*) is often overlooked. It is an incredibly tenacious plant, happy to climb, twisting and trailing its way over trees and walls, or to creep along the ground, making a lush evergreen carpet. It is so common and abundant that it is regarded by some as a nuisance. To others it is an ornamental haven for birds and bees, providing nectar and pollen into autumn and berries throughout winter. In the 'language of flowers', ivy signifies fidelity.

Skill level: INTERMEDIATE

Worked on 28 count linen, the finished cushion measures 46cm (18in) in diameter. Use 2 strands of cotton in the needle throughout and work each stitch over 2 fabric threads to give 14 stitches per 2.5cm (1in).

MATERIALS

To embroider the design:
- **Piece of 28 count cream evenweave linen, 49 x 49cm (19¼ x 19¼in), for the cushion front**
- **Stranded cotton embroidery threads as specified in the colour key**
- **Tapestry needle size 24 or 26**

To make up the cushion:
- **2 pieces of cream linen fabric, each 26 x 49cm (10¼ x 19¼in), for the cushion back**
- **150cm (59in) length of piping cord, covered with cream fabric**
- **30cm (12in) cream zip**
- **46cm (18in) circular cushion pad**
- **Basic sewing kit**

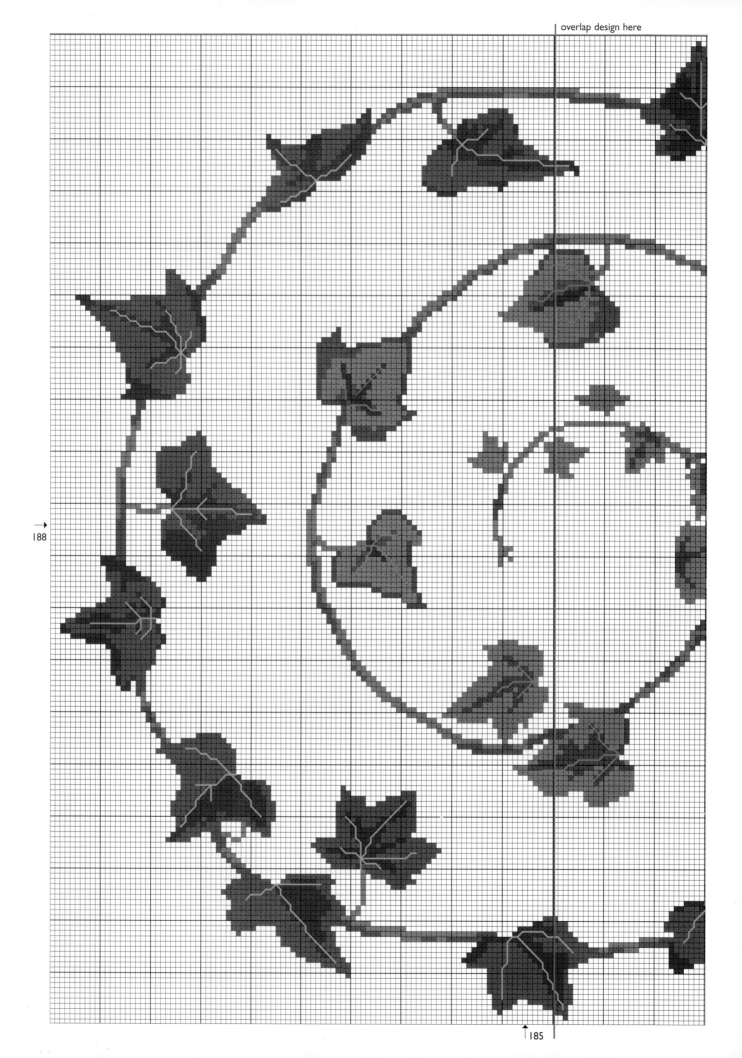

188

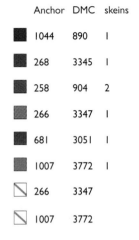

Anchor	DMC	skeins
1044	890	1
268	3345	1
258	904	2
266	3347	1
681	3051	1
1007	3772	1
266	3347	
1007	3772	

The overlap is marked
to make it easier to
work directly from the
book: it is not part of
the design.

**TO WORK THE
EMBROIDERY**

Start stitching at the centre of the design and in the centre of the fabric (see page 98). Progress outwards from the centre of the spiral, following the chart, until the stitching is complete. Finally, add the backstitched detail using 2 strands of cotton in the needle.

**TO MAKE UP THE
CUSHION**

To make a circular paper pattern with a diameter of 49cm (19¼in) including the seam allowance, follow the instructions that are given on page 108, pressing the drawing pin through the string 24.5cm (9⅝in) from the pencil.

The cushion is finished with a piped edge and a zip fastening (see pages 106 and 102). When the cover is complete, insert the cushion pad and close the zip.

variations

Individual leaf shapes can be arranged randomly on a cotton throw. Here smaller leaves have been chosen and embroidered using 11 count waste canvas (see page 97) for a chunky, homespun look that suits this slubby cotton throw. For a crisper and more refined look, choose the larger leaves and work them through 14 count waste canvas. Focus on the areas that will be seen most, perhaps grouping more leaves towards the edges of the throw and making them sparser towards the centre. Use scraps of green stranded cottons left over from other projects, as a variety of shades makes the design more interesting. Choose greens that are different enough from each other to show the markings on the leaves.

fossil appliqué

Valued for both the beauty of their form and the history they encapsulate, ammonite fossils have a spiral shape that makes an interesting subject for the natural room. This cushion cover incorporates an irregular pattern of ammonites, embroidered and appliquéd on to textured and frayed linens in understated browns and greys. A jute fringed edging echoes the frayed edges of the embroidered squares.

Ammonites were ancient sea creatures that dominated the deep waters of the oceans more than 300 million years ago. They grew by creating additional chambers of the same shape but each slightly larger than the last, resulting in their elegant spiral form. Each raised rib along the coil of a fossil represents the beginning of a new chamber.

Skill level: EASY

Worked on 27 count linen, the finished cushion measures 46 x 46cm (18 x 18in). Use 2 strands of cotton in the needle throughout, working each stitch over 2 fabric threads to give 13.5 stitches per 2.5cm (1in).

MATERIALS
To embroider the design:
- **5 pieces of 27 count natural evenweave linen, each 15 x 15cm (6 x 6in), for the appliqué patches**
- **Stranded cotton embroidery threads as specified in the colour key**
- **Tapestry needle size 24 or 26**

To make up the cushion:
- **Piece of taupe linen fabric, 49 x 49cm (19¼ x 19¼in), for the cushion front**
- **2 pieces of taupe linen fabric, 49 x 32cm (19¼ x 12½in), for the cushion back**
- **200cm (78¾in) length of fringed trimming**
- **3 buttons**
- **46cm (18in) square cushion pad**
- **Basic sewing kit**

TO WORK THE EMBROIDERY

Work one of the ammonite designs on each of the 5 evenweave linen squares, following the charts. Start stitching at the centre of the design and in the centre of the fabric square, and work outwards.

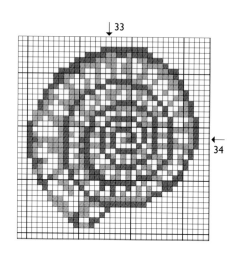

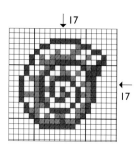

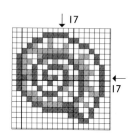

TO FINISH THE SQUARES

When all the squares have been stitched, trim the square with the largest design to 14 x 14cm (5½ x 5 ½in), the 2 with the medium-sized design to 13 x 13cm (5⅛ x 5⅛in), and the 2 with the smallest designs to 10 x 10cm (4 x 4in). Fray the perimeter of each square to a depth of about 1cm (⅜in) by carefully pulling out about 10 fabric threads across each edge. Oversew by hand around all the edges, catching the outer 2 or 3 threads of the square to prevent further fraying.

TO MAKE UP THE CUSHION

Lay the embroidered squares on to the cushion front, avoiding placing any close to the edges, and adjust them until you are happy with the arrangement. Pin and tack the squares into place, then hand or machine stitch them to the background fabric.

The cushion is finished with a fringe edging and a button fastening (see pages 107 and 104). When the cover is complete, insert the cushion pad and button up the cover.

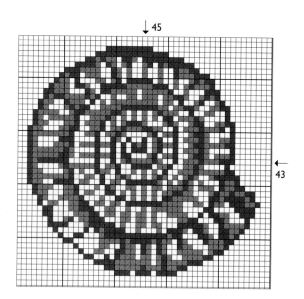

	Anchor	DMC	skeins
■	273	645	1
▨	1040	647	1
▦	904	3787	1
▨	392	642	1

variations

The shape of ammonite fossils has such precision and beauty that these designs would make an interesting series of pictures, mounted in plain wooden frames. Here the smallest ammonite design adds interesting pattern and texture to a plain lampshade. There is not much contrast between the colours of the natural calico shade and the linen squares, but when the light is turned on it shines through the shade and the squares appear in silhouette, highlighting the open, meshy weave of the linen with its frayed edges.

sea shells

Shells have beautiful architectural structures in an array of sea-washed colours. This design incorporates the distinctive purple-black curves of the mussel, the spiral forms of the tower shell and whelk, the flat fan-like scallop and the paper-thin shell of the common tellin delicately tinged with pink. These are set against pleats of the palest grey-blue silk to evoke waves lapping ashore.

Shells give protection and support to the creatures that they enclose. These crystallized calcium carbonate structures are based on a few relatively simple shapes – the coil, the cone or mirrored halves hinged together to form one shell. Their colour depends on the food consumed by the creature and the environment outside the shell.

Skill level: ADVANCED

Worked on silk through 14 count waste canvas, giving 14 stitches per 2.5cm (1in), the finished cushion measures 46 x 46cm (18 x 18in). Use 2 strands of cotton in the needle throughout.

MATERIALS

To embroider the design:
- **Piece of grey-blue silk fabric, 97 x 49cm (38¼ x 19¼in), for the cushion front**
- **Piece of 14 count waste canvas, 49 x 16cm (19¼ x 6¼in)**
- **Stranded cotton embroidery threads as specified in the colour key**
- **Tapestry needle size 24 or 26**

To make up the cushion:
- **2 pieces of grey-blue silk fabric, each 49 x 32cm (19¼ x 12½in), for the cushion back**
- **3 buttons**
- **46cm (18in) square cushion pad**
- **Basic sewing kit**

TO MAKE THE PLEATS

Make the pleats first, so that the shell motifs can be positioned accurately between them. Lay out the fabric for the cushion front, right side up. Using tailor's chalk, mark a 1.5cm (⅝in) seam allowance along one of the shorter edges; then measure and mark the stitching lines all the way down the fabric, finishing with a 1.5cm (⅝in) seam allowance at the other end (1). Alternatively, you could mark the ends of the stitching lines only, to minimize the amount of tailor's chalk on the fabric.

Each pleat is 2cm (¾in) wide to the fold, when complete. Starting with the first pleat, fold the fabric with wrong sides together, matching the stitching lines, and press in a sharp crease along the fold. Repeat this for the rest of the pleats. Sew a line of stitching along the stitching line or between the stitching-line marks, parallel with the crease, to form each pleat (2). Press all the pleats to the left, using a damp cloth to achieve sharp edges to the folds without scorching the fabric (3).

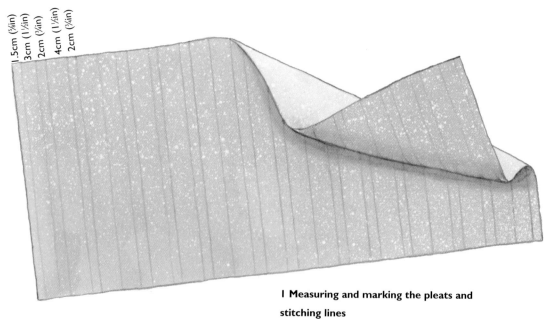

1.5cm (⅝in)
3cm (1⅛in)
2cm (¾in)
4cm (1½in)
2cm (¾in)

1 Measuring and marking the pleats and stitching lines

2 Stitching the pleats

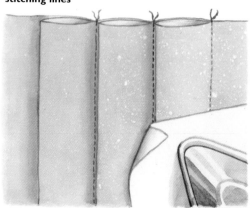

3 Pressing the finished pleats to the left

TO WORK THE EMBROIDERY

Cut 4 strips of waste canvas each 21 squares wide by 49cm (19¼in) long and tack them in the 4cm (1½in) gaps between the pleats. Fold the fabric in half across the pleats to find the centre line, and for each column of shells line up the centre point marked on the chart with this horizontal centre line. Work 5 design repeats centrally within the 4cm (1½in) gaps between the pleats, in the order indicated below the chart (see page 97 for details on working with waste canvas).

TO MAKE UP THE CUSHION

The cushion is finished with a plain seamed edge and a button fastening (see pages 105 and 104). When the cover is complete, insert the cushion pad and button up the cover.

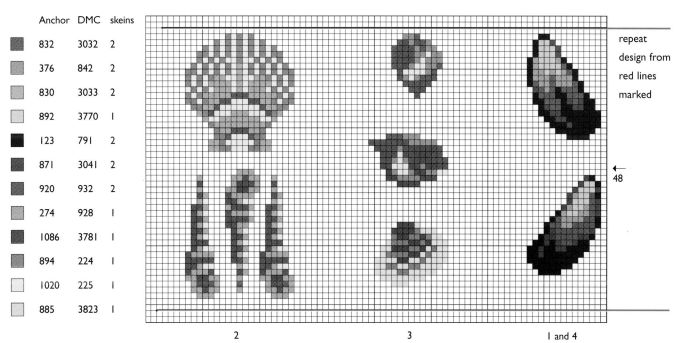

Anchor	DMC	skeins
832	3032	2
376	842	2
830	3033	2
892	3770	1
123	791	2
871	3041	2
920	932	2
274	928	1
1086	3781	1
894	224	1
1020	225	1
885	3823	1

repeat design from red lines marked

← 48

2   3   1 and 4

variations

Any of the shell motifs in this design could be used individually or in groups on towels or curtains for the bathroom. This white cotton laundry bag has been embroidered with a scallop flanked by tower shells, using 2 strands of cotton worked through 14 count waste canvas. For a larger shell, work with 3 strands of cotton through 11 count waste canvas (for example, the scallop would increase in height from 2.5cm/1in to 3.5cm/1⅜in). Try working the designs on unbleached, textured fabrics for a more rugged, windswept beach look. Shells could even be worked through waste canvas along the edges of a cotton rag rug.

patchwork hellebore

A blocked border pattern reflects the range of greens in the saucer-shaped flowers of the hellebore that it surrounds. Green promotes harmony and balance, and there are not many flowers that are as truly green as this one. The theme of a simple blocked pattern is continued in the patchwork of plain, printed and woven fabrics, which draw together the different tones and textures of other soft furnishings within the room.

The hellebore belongs to the Ranunculaceae family, which also includes the buttercup. It is one of the first flowers of the year, appearing in late winter or very early spring. An evergreen perennial, it prefers the moist semi-shade of woodlands.

Skill level: EASY

Worked on 11 count Aida, giving 11 stitches per 2.5cm (1in), the finished cushion measures 41 x 41cm (16 x 16in). Use 3 strands of cotton in the needle throughout.

MATERIALS
To embroider the design:
- **Piece of 11 count white Aida, 20 x 20cm (7⅞ x 7⅞in), for the central panel of the cushion front**
- **20 pieces of 11 count white Aida, each 8.6 x 8.6cm (3⅜ x 3⅜in)**
- **Stranded cotton embroidery threads as specified in the colour key**
- **Tapestry needle size 24 or 26**

To make up the cushion:
- **20 pieces of assorted cream and green fabrics, each 8.6 x 8.6cm (3⅜ x 3⅜in)**
- **2 pieces of toning fabric, each 44 x 29.5cm (17¼ x 11⅝in), for the cushion back**
- **170cm (67in) length of cream piping**
- **3 buttons**
- **41cm (16in) square cushion pad**
- **Basic sewing kit**

TO WORK THE EMBROIDERY

First stitch the border that surrounds the central panel. Begin at one of the corners, 1.5cm (⅝in) in from both the horizontal and vertical edges of the fabric. Then use the border in combination with the chart to position and stitch the flower correctly inside it. In the centre of each of the Aida squares for the patchwork, stitch a single block of colour 3 stitches by 3 stitches. Colours from the design were chosen at random for the blocks.

	Anchor	DMC	skeins
	292	3078	1
	259	772	1
	261	368	1
	262	3363	1
	878	501	1

TO MAKE UP THE CUSHION

Mark a sewing line 1.5cm (⅝in) in from the edge on the reverse of each square, so that they will be a consistent size and join neatly at the corners when stitched together. Lay out all the patchwork pieces, alternating the Aida squares with the other fabric squares. Try to achieve a balance of colour with a good mix of dark and light, patterned and plain. There should always be an Aida square opposite a fabric square and all the seams should line up with each other.

When you are satisfied with the arrangement, begin to stitch the squares into strips either by hand or by machine. Join the squares with right sides facing and stitch on the sewing line (1), then press the seams open. Make 4 strips of 3 squares each for above and below the central panel, then stitch these strips together (2) into 2 blocks of 6 squares, each 3 squares wide by 2 squares deep. Make 4 strips of 7 squares each for the sides of the central panel, then stitch these strips into 2 blocks of 14 squares, each 2 squares wide by 7 squares deep. Stitch the smaller blocks above and below the central panel, then the larger blocks on either side.

The cushion is finished with a piped edge and a button fastening (see pages 106 and 104). When the cover is complete, insert the cushion pad and button up the cover.

variations

This simple block design is reminiscent of mosaic tiles, making it ideal as an edging on towels or a blind in the kitchen or bathroom. The blocked border design adds colour to the edge of a plain white hand towel trimmed with fresh white and yellow daisies. The cross stitch was worked through 11 count waste canvas, with 3 strands of cotton in the needle. It would be equally effective in shades of blue and turquoise.

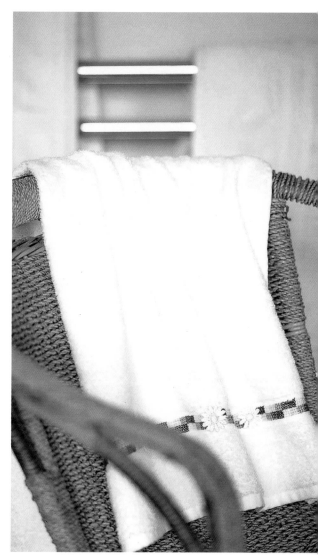

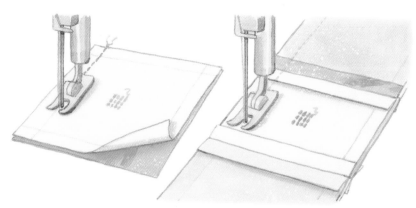

1 Joining the squares into strips

2 Joining the strips into blocks

the rich room

Richness is perceived by all of our senses – in fragrant aromas, mellow sounds, vivid colours, full textures and flavourful tastes. The rich room, incorporating these, will be a place for private relaxation and self-indulgence or somewhere inviting to welcome others, a place for socializing and entertaining.

The colours of North Africa, India and the Orient are the obvious places to look for inspiration. Like a global magpie, you can collect 'jewels' from different countries – rich ruby-red, garnet and a touch of gold from India; deep terracotta, the colour of *tadlekt* (mud) walls, from Morocco; and regal purple, midnight blue and emerald green from the silks of the East. These colours, and some of the styling, can be adapted to suit the architecture around us.

Inspiration can also be found closer to home. The forest holds an incredibly rich palette of greens, with fir, moss and olive giving way to copper, burnt umber and nut-brown in autumn. From the earth itself come some of the first pigments to be discovered – ochre, umber and sienna. In addition, the rich colours of food and drink could inspire the colours for a dining room. Choose from berry, damson, aubergine and the deep claret colour of vintage wine.

You may be able to derive inspiration from an ornately carved and painted tea table, an intricate cedar fretworked screen or a beautifully decorated chest to set the style of a whole room... The rich room also needs a display of flamboyant fresh flowers in dramatic colours with strong scents.

Textured papers with embossed and velvet pile designs provide subtle patterning on walls, particularly as the depth of the texture is emphasized by shadow. However, this is best confined to selected areas such as a window recess and contrasted with simpler surfaces. Gilded stars or squares can be magnificently dramatic on walls in deep, rich colours. Lustrous metallic finishes on ornamental plasterwork and architectural mouldings bring out their three-dimensional qualities.

If walls are painted in a dark colour, painting the ceiling cream or white will prevent all the light being absorbed and the room becoming too dark. Fabric banners in exotic colours and patterns are more than wall coverings – they can also be a work of art. Some of the most interesting banners are created using inspired choices of fabrics from unusual sources. Sari fabrics, with decorative metallic edgings and rich colours that border on bright, make beautiful, glistening banners.

In hotter climates tiled and brick floors are popular because they are cooling, but a similar look can still be created for colder climates by using warmer materials. A terracotta-coloured wool carpet will provide the same rich colour as tiles while proving much warmer underfoot, and the interlocking pattern of parquet is similar to that of bricks. A floor strewn with tactile, thick tufted rugs not only encourages barefoot living but can also bring colour and pattern into a room without being overwhelming. Persian knotted-wool rugs come with stylized motifs on a deeply coloured base – usually red and blue – and they are said to improve in

appearance as they become worn. Woollen kelims and cotton dhurries are both flat weaves which are available in a fantastic variety of designs, different sizes and many colour combinations.

You may be able to derive inspiration from an ornately carved and painted tea table, an intricate cedar fretworked screen or a beautifully decorated chest to set the style of a whole room. Adapt existing furniture by painting it in rich dark browns, reds or even black, like the glossy lacquerwork of Japan. Something as simple as changing the handles on cupboards and drawers can completely change the character of a piece.

Nothing is more welcoming than the warm glow of a flame. If a roaring open fire is not practical, candles and lanterns will touch the surroundings with their magical light. They can also bring fragrance to the room. Rose and jasmine oils in a burner release a subtle perfume, while sticks or coils of burning incense create a more heady aroma.

Collections of interesting items and pieces of personal significance, grouped together by type or colour, can make wonderful displays. Mosaics, bejewelled boxes, glazed pottery and coloured glass form a tapestry of colour that creates a focal point and sets a style. The rich room also needs a display of flamboyant fresh flowers in dramatic colours with strong scents. Gladioli, oriental lilies and orchids make wonderful cut flowers, exotic blooms, such as hibiscus and passion flower, can be grown indoors.

Soft furnishings are essential in making the rich room a comfort zone. A cashmere throw is the epitome of luxurious softness hidden behind an understated appearance, while generous quantities of soft furnishings made from velvets, silks and satins create a sumptuous setting. Swathes of fabric can be further embellished with beads, fringes, tassels, braids and cords for a touch of unashamed extravagance. Rugs and throws in layers of colour, texture and pattern can create a comfortable, welcoming sofa.

The embroidery designs for the rich room are inspired by the hot reds of chilli peppers, the rich golden-oranges of autumn leaves, the graceful commanding shape of the gladiolus and shimmering rainbow colours from a peacock feather. They incorporate richly coloured and textured fabrics – velvet, silk, chenille and organza in crimson, purple, amber and rich peat brown. Basic fabrics, too, can be transformed by embroidery and, with the help of braids and trimmings, made into extravagant cushions.

rich

organza leaf

The autumn landscape provides an inspirational colour palette for the rich room. The delicate shape of the deeply lobed Japanese maple leaf is interpreted here in shimmering organza outlined in warm, earthy tones. It is worked on a background of amber chenille, and the cushion is finished with a generous organza edging to create a combination of luxurious textures and glowing colours.

The Japanese maple (*Acer palmatum*) is a member of the Aceraceae family, whose species and cultivars have many different leaf shapes and are particularly colourful in autumn. These outstandingly beautiful small trees are the cornerstone of Japanese gardening.

Skill level: ADVANCED

Worked through 11 count waste canvas, giving 11 stitches per 2.5cm (1in), the finished cushion measures 46 x 46cm (18 x 18in), plus a 5cm (2in) Oxford border. Use 3 strands of cotton in the needle throughout.

MATERIALS
To embroider the design:
• **Piece of 11 count waste canvas, 32 x 32cm (12½ x 12½in)**
• **Piece of brown organza fabric, 32 x 32cm (12½ x 12½in)**
• **Piece of amber chenille fabric, 49 x 49cm (19¼ x 19¼in), for the cushion front**
• **Stranded cotton embroidery threads as specified in the colour key**
• **Tapestry needle size 24 or 26**

To make up the cushion:
• **2 pieces of amber chenille fabric, 49 x 26cm (19¼ x 10¼in), for the cushion back**
• **4 strips each of amber chenille and brown organza fabrics, each 8 x 60cm (3⅛ x 23⅝in), for the edging**
• **30cm (12in) amber zip**
• **46cm (18in) square cushion pad**
• **Basic sewing kit**

TO WORK THE EMBROIDERY

Tack the organza square, with the waste canvas on top, in the centre of the cushion front, right sides up. Work the leaf outline in cross stitch, through all 3 layers. When stitching is complete, unpick the tacking and remove the waste canvas (see page 97 for details on working with waste canvas). Using a pair of sharp embroidery scissors, trim back the organza as close to the cross-stitched outline as possible without damaging the stitching.

TO MAKE UP THE CUSHION

Complete the back of the cushion by inserting the zip fastening (see page 102), before adding the border. Pin, tack and stitch the organza border strips to the 4 edges of the front centre panel, taking a 1.5cm (⅝in)

seam allowance and folding the previous strip back out of the way as you go. Start and stop stitching 1.5cm (⅝in) from the ends of the fabric. To mitre the corners, draw a straight line at a 45 degree angle from the corner point of the stitching on the centre panel to the outer edge of the strip (1). Bring the strip that was underneath to the top and repeat the process (2). These 2 lines indicate the stitching line. Match them together, with right sides facing, then pin, tack and stitch along the line, starting at the inner point and working to the outer edge (3). Repeat the process for the other 3 corners. Press the seams open for a neat finish (4). Repeat the whole process for the back panel, using the chenille fabric strips.

To complete the cushion, follow the instructions for making an Oxford or single flanged border (see page 106), locating the inner line of stitching on top of the border seam. Topstitch around the outer edge of the border for a crisp finish. When the cover is complete, insert the cushion pad and close the zip.

1 Drawing a 45 degree angle for the mitre

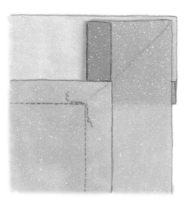

2 Repeating the process with the lower strip

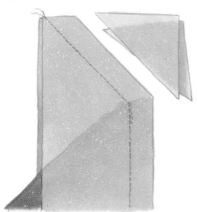

3 Pinning and stitching the mitre

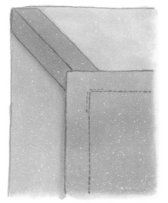

4 Pressing the seam open for a neat finish

	Anchor	DMC	skeins
■	359	801	1
■	22	3777	1
■	341	918	1
■	1003	721	1

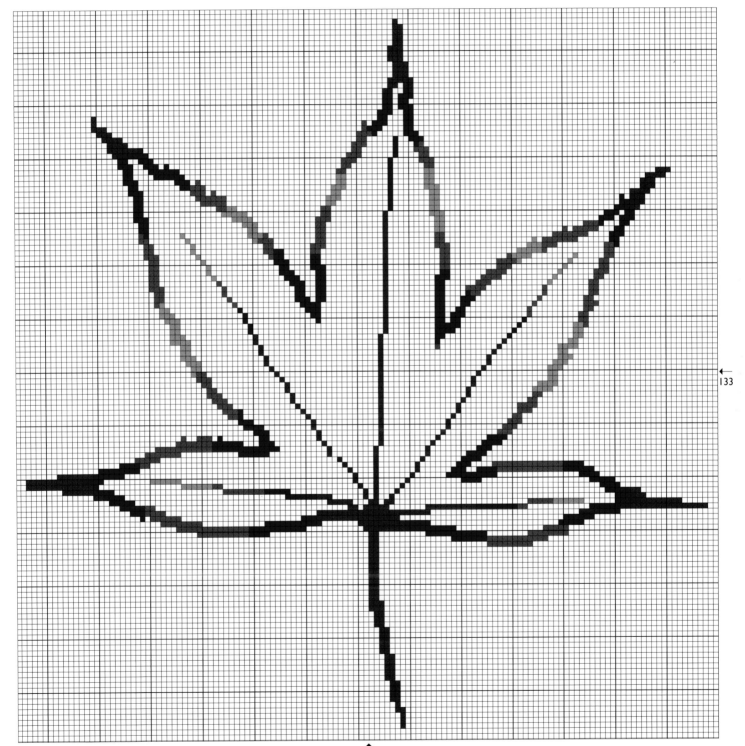

↑ 132

← 133

variations

Simply by using different types of fabric, the look of
this cushion will be transformed. Replacing the
organza with a richly coloured cotton check creates a
cover with a homespun, country look. Putting fabrics
of the same colour but with differently textured
surfaces against each other and stitching the outline
in the same single colour gives a subtle twist to the
design. Try brushed cotton on crisp linen or velvet on
corduroy. The corner of this throw has been
embroidered with a drift of smaller leaves, in shades
of amethyst, cinnabar and copper. They were worked
in scraps of woollen yarn. The line of stitching that
forms these smaller shapes is quite fine, so if you wish
to use them to create outlines around a contrast
fabric (as in the main project) use a fabric that does
not fray, such as felt.

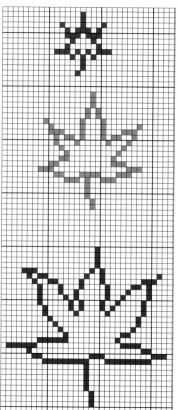

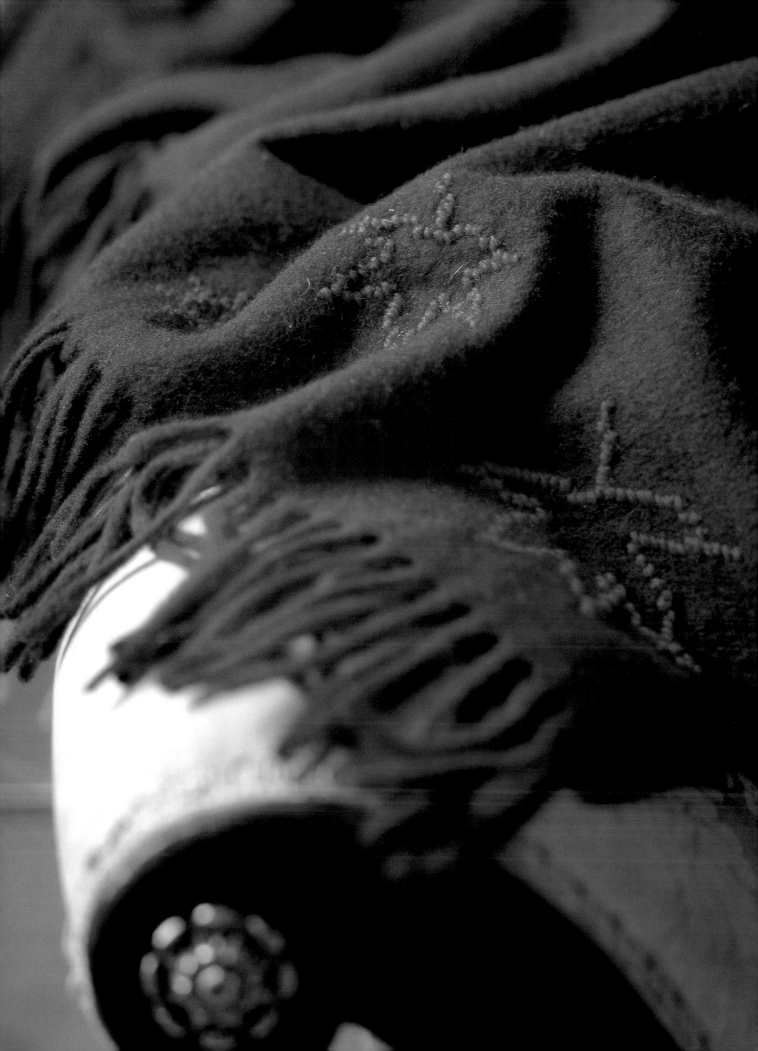

chilli peppers

Red is a fiery colour, and lightened by golden-yellow it creates sumptuously inviting soft furnishings. The chilli pepper has come out of the kitchen and in this design lends its heat and colour to a crimson velvet bolster cushion. Traditionally used on day beds and *chaise longues*, bolsters offer support for other cushions. They soften a sofa, particularly one with a very upright back, and are perfect for lounging on a bed or on the floor.

The chilli pepper (*Capsicum annuum*), which is a relative of both the potato and the tomato, originated in Mexico and Central America. More than three centuries of cultivation have resulted in a range of varieties differing in shape, size, flavour and pungency. An essential ingredient of many cuisines, from India to Mexico, chilli is renowned for its hot, spicy taste.

Skill level: INTERMEDIATE

Worked on 28 count evenweave fabric, the finished bolster measures 52cm (20½in) in length. Use 3 strands of cotton in the needle throughout, working each stitch over 3 fabric threads to give 9½ stitches per 2.5cm (1in).

MATERIALS
To embroider the design:
• **2 strips of 28 count golden-yellow cotton-mix evenweave fabric, each 49 x 14cm (19¼ x 5½in)**
• **Stranded cotton embroidery threads as specified in the colour key**
• **Tapestry needle size 24 or 26**

To make up the bolster:
• **Piece of red velvet, 49 x 55cm (19¼ x 21⅝in)**
• **200cm (78¾in) length of red-and-gold braid**
• **2 strips of red velvet, each 49 x 10cm (19¼ x 4in)**
• **100cm (39½in) length of piping cord, covered with red velvet**
• **2 self-cover buttons with scraps of red velvet to cover them**
• **40cm (15¾in) red zip**
• **Fabric to make the bolster inner, 49 x 55cm (19¼ x 21⅝in) plus 2 circles radius 7.3cm (2⅞in)**
• **Fleecy polyester filling**
• **Basic sewing kit**

TO WORK THE EMBROIDERY

Follow the charted design, starting 1.5cm (⅝in) in from the end of the fabric strip. Work 4 repeats along each strip. As this is a repeating design, the first line follows on from the last and the pattern will flow.

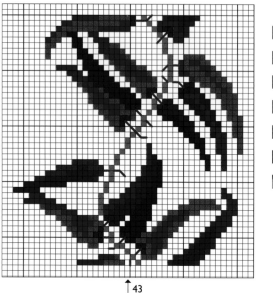

	Anchor	DMC	skeins
■	897	902	2
■	20	816	2
■	47	304	2
■	1098	666	2
■	1049	301	1
■	246	986	1
◩	246	986	

↑ 43

TO MAKE UP THE CUSHION

With the right sides of all the pieces facing upwards, position the 2 embroidered strips on the large piece of red velvet, 5cm (2in) in from the ends. Pin, tack and then secure the strips in place with a line of stitching down each side. Hand sew the braid invisibly over the lines of stitching and covering the raw edges of the embroidered strips. Now follow the instructions for making a bolster cushion on page 109.

variations

Chilli peppers can be put in the more traditional setting of the kitchen. For bright, *cantina*-style dining, embroider them on a green checked tablecloth and napkins. Following the more exotic style, a larger pepper has been embroidered on this organza and silk drawstring purse, stitched through 11 count waste canvas, using 3 strands of cotton and incorporating a metallic blending filament.

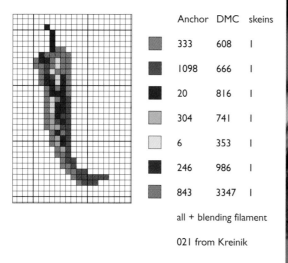

	Anchor	DMC	skeins
	333	608	1
	1098	666	1
	20	816	1
	304	741	1
	6	353	1
	246	986	1
	843	3347	1

all + blending filament

021 from Kreinik

peacock and jewel

This embroidery interprets the shimmering colours of a peacock feather by incorporating a metallic blending filament with stranded cotton to create the characteristic combination of intense colour and subtle shimmer. The iridescent beaded trim around the edge of the cushion adds to the jewel-like effect.

The peacock has strutted in the gardens of kings and emperors since biblical times, raising his feathers in a display unsurpassed for drama and beauty. In China during the T'ang dynasty peacocks were so highly valued that their feathers decorated royal processions. The peacock and its plumage have been portrayed by artists through the ages and never more beautifully than in art nouveau glass and ceramics.

Skill level: ADVANCED

Worked on 14 count Aida, giving 14 stitches per 2.5cm (1in), the finished cushion measures 41 x 41cm (16 x 16in). Use 2 strands of cotton in the needle throughout, plus a single strand of blending filament as indicated.

MATERIALS

To embroider the design:
- **Piece of 14 count navy blue Aida, 44 x 44cm (17¼ x 17¼in)**
- **Stranded cotton embroidery threads and Kreinik blending filament as specified in the colour key**
- **Tapestry needle size 24 or 26**

To make up the cushion:
- **2 pieces of navy blue velvet, each 44 x 23.5cm (17¼ x 9¼in), for the cushion back**
- **170cm (67in) length of beaded fringe trim**
- **30cm (12in) navy blue zip**
- **41cm (16in) square cushion pad**
- **Basic sewing kit**

TO WORK THE EMBROIDERY

Begin by working the border. Sew a baseline in running stitch to assist in achieving correct alignment of the design. Start stitching the baseline at the corner, 5cm (2in) in from both the horizontal and vertical edges of the fabric, and count 186 fabric squares before turning each corner. See page 98 for instructions on how to thread the needle when combining different types of thread. Stitch the outlines of the teardrops first to get the spacing correct, which is particularly important in border designs such as this to ensure that the end of the design meets the beginning. Once you have plotted the outlines correctly, fill them in. Position the feather by referring to the chart and aligning it with the border.

TO MAKE UP THE CUSHION

The cushion is finished with an iridescent beaded fringe and a zip fastening (see pages 107 and 102). When the cover is complete, insert the cushion pad and close the zip.

baseline

baseline

variations

A very simplified version of the border design, using just the teardrop outline, would be quick to work. It would make a subtle edge detail, with echoes of Indian paisleys, along the hem of a curtain. The corner sections of the teardrop border can be combined to create a flower-like motif. Here it has been embroidered on a deep blue velvet seat cover, creating a lovely contrast of textures combined with intense colour. It was stitched with 2 strands of cotton in the needle, through 14 count waste canvas.

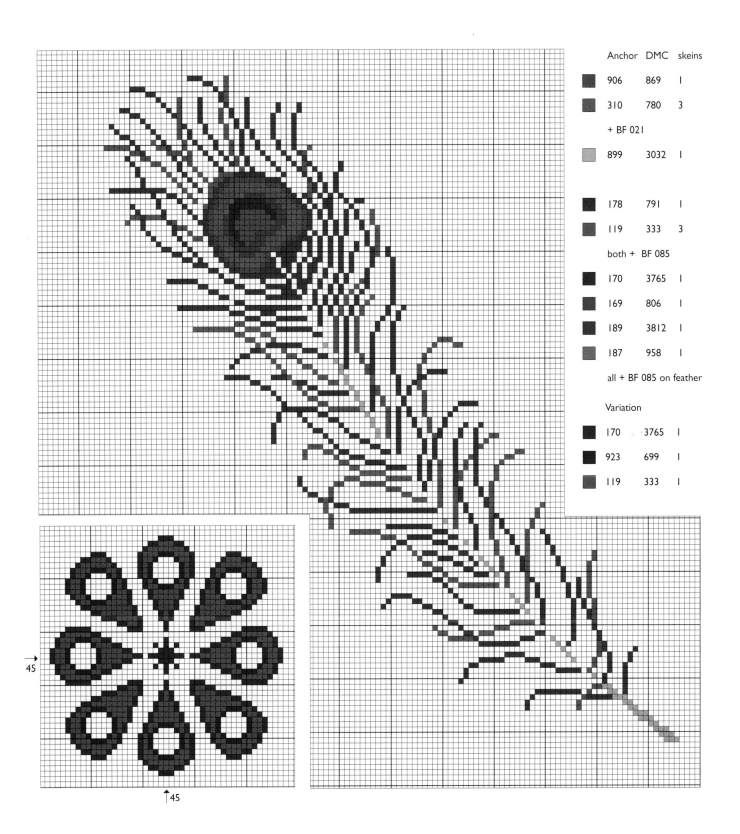

Anchor	DMC	skeins
906	869	1
310	780	3
+ BF 021		
899	3032	1
178	791	1
119	333	3
both + BF 085		
170	3765	1
169	806	1
189	3812	1
187	958	1
all + BF 085 on feather		

Variation

Anchor	DMC	skeins
170	3765	1
923	699	1
119	333	1

45

↑ 45

gladiolus

The gladiolus in this design has a single spike of funnel-shaped flowers and pointed leaves that create a graceful silhouette, and it is embroidered in an unusual mix of reds and greens on purple and gold. The shimmering surface of plain shot silk changes colour depending on the angle of view, giving the design added richness and depth.

The name gladiolus is derived from the Latin word *gladius*, meaning sword. The plant is also sometimes called the sword lily because of its distinctive narrow, pointed leaves. Although originally from Africa, the gladiolus was introduced to Europe in the late 17th century. In the 'language of flowers', it signifies strength of character.

Skill level: INTERMEDIATE

Worked through 14 count waste canvas, giving 14 stitches per 2.5cm (1in), the finished cushion measures 65 x 30cm (25½ x 12in). Use 2 strands of cotton in the needle throughout.

MATERIALS

To work the embroidery:
- **Piece of purple silk fabric, 52 x 33cm (20½ x 13in), for the cushion front**
- **Piece of 14 count waste canvas, 8 x 38cm (3⅛ x 15in)**
- **Stranded cotton embroidery threads as specified in the colour key**
- **Tapestry needle size 24 or 26**

To make up the cushion:
- **2 pieces of purple silk fabric, each 52 x 18cm (20½ x 7in), for the cushion back**
- **4 pieces of gold silk fabric, each 33 x 11cm (13 x 4¼in)**
- **30cm (12in) purple zip**
- **65 x 30cm (25½ x 12in) cushion pad**
- **Basic sewing kit**

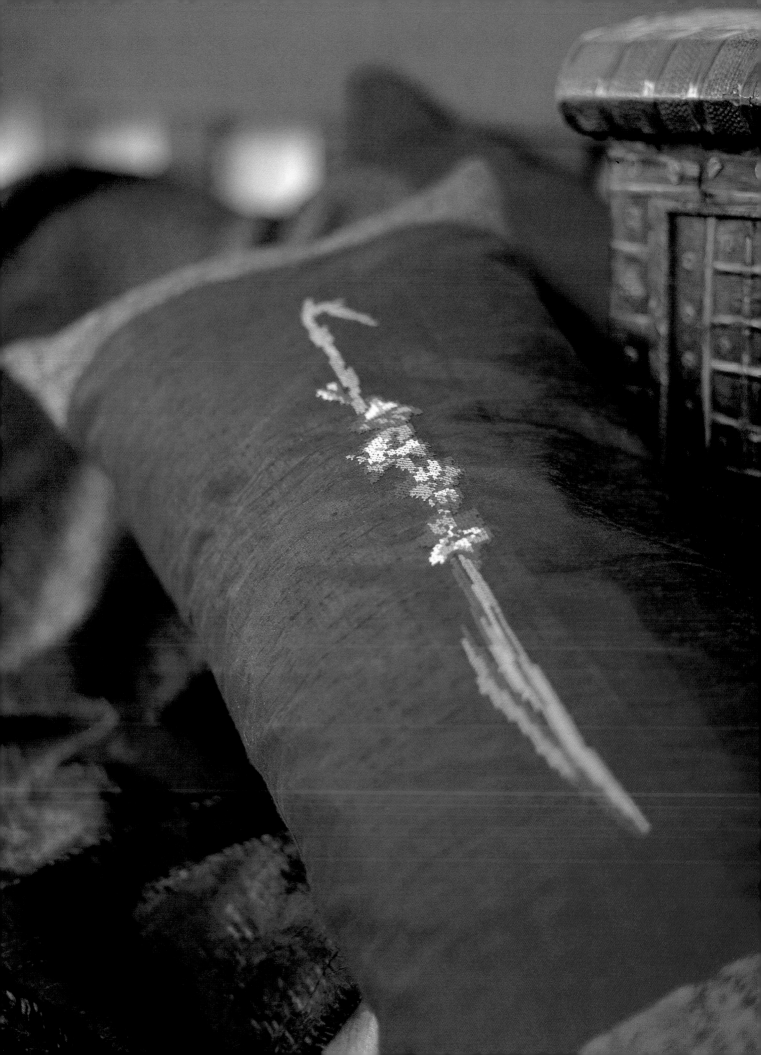

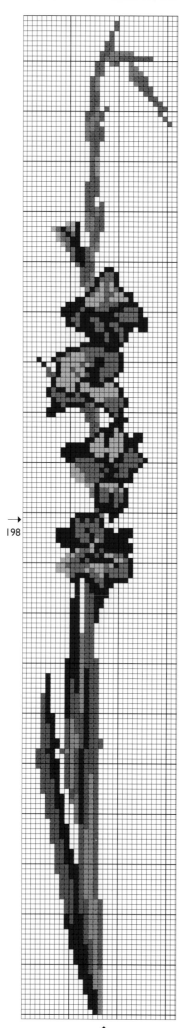

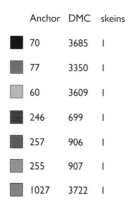

Anchor	DMC	skeins
70	3685	1
77	3350	1
60	3609	1
246	699	1
257	906	1
255	907	1
1027	3722	1

198 →

↑28

TO WORK THE EMBROIDERY

Tack the waste canvas in place centrally on the purple silk fabric and work the design following the chart (see page 97 for details on working with waste canvas).

TO MAKE UP THE CUSHION

Insert the zip between the 2 back sections of purple silk (see page 102), then stitch the gold silk panels to the ends of the cushion front and back, taking a 1.5cm (⅝in) seam allowance. Press the seams open, then stitch the front and back together with a plain seamed edge (see page 105). When the cover is complete, insert the cushion pad and close the zip.

variations

Embroidering 3 or 4 flower spikes lengthways on a bolster cushion and a single spike on an accompanying throw would look very dramatic and luxurious. The gladiolus makes a striking picture because of its distinctive outline. Here it has been embroidered on a golden-yellow evenweave fabric and mounted in a richly coloured mosaic frame. Anchor 70, 77 and 60 are replaced with Anchor 102, 111 and 109 (DMC 550, 208 and 209), respectively. The rest of the colours remain the same.

the bright room

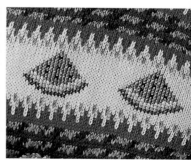

Bright colour exudes natural energy and power. It elevates the spirit, inspiring positivity and exciting the senses. Bright colours in the entrance hall welcome guests; they make the kitchen a place of hospitality, and in the dining room they promote the enjoyment of food and conversation.

Nature is the strongest inspiration for combining bright colours. Flowers have evolved in vivid shades to shout the message of pollination to the birds and bees, resulting in daring contrasts and riotous colour. Think of china-blue speedwell self-sown alongside lime-green lady's mantle and of sunny yellow cowslips growing among bluebells. Throughout the world cultures are strongly influenced by their natural surroundings. In the Caribbean islands the clarity of light intensifies the brilliance of the colours of the sand, sea and lush foliage, which in turn is reflected in the use of strong colours in the decoration of houses, handicrafts and textiles. Sunflower-yellow with the strong pink of bougainvillea is a recurring theme in the Mexican home, while in Greece intense azure-blue and dazzling white are the primary elements of style. Bold colour also became popular in cooler climates from the late 1950s, and it was the advent of new materials, plastics in particular, that was the inspiration.

bright

Paint is the most versatile of decorating materials as it can be used to create flat colour, textured effects, stripes and blocks, and freehand or stencilled patterns. Mistakes are easily remedied, so enjoy being daring with your use of painted colour, but always bear in mind that walls represent a large surface area within a room, and the colour they are painted is proportionately powerful. Bright colours have great dramatic potential because their rawness gives them instant impact and immensely strong character. Walls can be doused in saturated colour, but they can also be a less dominant element within a room. Painted in a neutral shade, they provide a foil that accentuates brilliant, deeply coloured furnishings and accessories.

Colour is a wonderful tool, which can be used to change the way we perceive space. A block or band of bold colour on one wall can visually change the dimensions of a room and draw the eye towards, or away from, certain

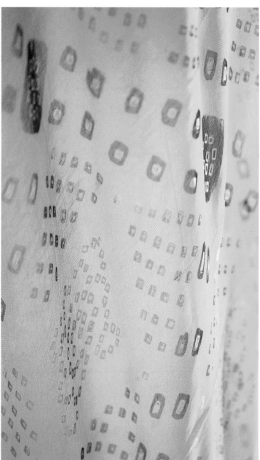

bright

Colour is a wonderful tool, which can be used to change the way we perceive space. A block or band of bold colour on one wall can visually change the dimensions of a room and draw the eye towards, or away from, certain features.

features. Colour can highlight existing architectural detail, such as an arch or ceiling rose, and where a room has little such detail the colour will introduce character and spirit.

Natural floors work well in a bright environment (for more detail see page 10). Partnered with natural colours, the overall effect of bright colours need not be overwhelming. Fitted carpets in dramatic, solid colours, like midnight blue or deepest red, provide a bold background plane that will also lead the eye right to the edges of the room, making it appear bigger. The bright splash of colour that a rug provides can pull a room together and add focus.

Uncovered windows brighten a small room, making maximum use of natural light to intensify a bright colour scheme. Bright colours change dramatically with changes of light, being intense in daylight but becoming richer in the evening. Window frames can be painted in a lively colour to frame the view.

Bright colours are theatrical and accessories can add to the drama. A colourful Chinese lantern hung at the window, a magnificent print on the wall or a bead curtain will enliven and personalize a room. Whether you choose a few items of glassware, carefully placed and interestingly lit, or turn a corner of the room into an Aladdin's cave of junk-shop finds, will depend on your personality.

Soft furnishings can introduce and combine colours in a way more difficult on larger areas. Embroidery makes an opportunity to unite colours in a room and introduce decorative pattern to soft furnishings, without being overpowering.

flower power

Flowers provide a never-ending source of inspiration for design and colour in the home. In this design the flowerheads have been freed from their vases and scattered on a white linen cushion. Their intense colours are captured perfectly in thread.

     Iris was the messenger of the gods of the Ancient Greek and the origin of the fleur-de-lis. In the 'language of flowers', anemone means forsaken and helianthus signifies adoration.

Skill level: INTERMEDIATE

Worked on 27 count evenweave linen, the finished cushion measures 46 x 46cm (18 x 18in). Use 2 strands of cotton in the needle throughout, working each stitch over 2 fabric threads to give 13.5 stitches per 2.5cm (1in).

MATERIALS
To embroider the design:
- **Piece of 27 count white linen evenweave fabric, 49 x 49cm (19¼ x 19¼in), for the cushion front**
- **Stranded cotton embroidery threads as specified on the colour key**
- **Tapestry needle size 24 or 26**

To make up the cushion:
- **2 pieces of colour-matched cotton or linen fabric, each 49 x 32cm (19¼ x 12½in)**
- **200cm (78in) length of piping cord, covered with white fabric**
- **3 buttons**
- **46cm (18in) square cushion pad**
- **Basic sewing kit**

TO WORK THE
EMBROIDERY

Decide roughly where the flowers are to be placed on the cushion cover by referring to the photograph opposite. Leave at least 7.5cm (3in) clearance from the edge of the fabric so that they are not hidden around the sides of the cushion once the pad is inserted. Mark squares on the fabric in running stitch for each flower, then work the designs within the appropriate squares. When all the flowers are complete, remove the running-stitch markers.

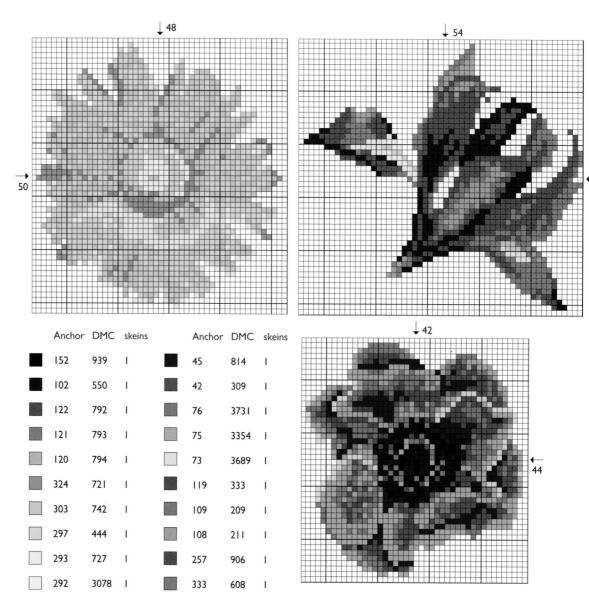

	Anchor	DMC	skeins		Anchor	DMC	skeins
■	152	939	1	■	45	814	1
■	102	550	1	■	42	309	1
■	122	792	1	■	76	3731	1
■	121	793	1	■	75	3354	1
■	120	794	1	■	73	3689	1
■	324	721	1	■	119	333	1
■	303	742	1	■	109	209	1
■	297	444	1	■	108	211	1
■	293	727	1	■	257	906	1
■	292	3078	1	■	333	608	1

TO MAKE UP THE
CUSHION

The cushion is finished with a piped edge and a button back (see instructions on pages 106 and 104). When the cover is complete, insert the pad and button up the cover.

variations

For a cushion with a simpler design, which focuses on a single colour area, for instance oranges and yellows or blues and purples, embroider one of the large flowers at the centre of the cushion and surround it with a scattering of smaller flowers. Use any of the flowers individually as motifs for embroidery. The yellow helianthus would make a fine centrepiece on a sunny yellow tablecloth. Calming blue delphinium florets embroidered on crisp white bedlinen will introduce understated detail to a restful bedroom. This pillowslip was stitched with 2 strands of cotton in the needle, through 14 count waste canvas.

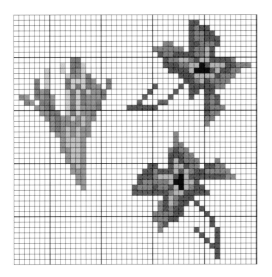

tropical knit

Richly patterned textiles and succulent, refreshing fruit capture the exuberance and vitality of the Caribbean. Hot pink embroidered watermelons are set against a colourful knitted jacquard design. The cushion is trimmed with tassels that pick up colours from the design.

   The watermelon (*Citrullus lanatus*) originated in Africa, probably in the Nile valley, but it is now widespread throughout the tropics. Encased in a deep green skin, its pink pulp is scattered with large, dark seeds and oozes with sugary-sweet juice – food and drink in one. Botanically, the plant is actually classified as an annual herb.

Skill level: ADVANCED

Worked in double knitting yarn on 3¾mm (No 9/US 4) needles, the finished cushion measures 41 x 41cm (16 x 16in).

MATERIALS

To embroider the design:
- **Double knitting (DK) yarn and stranded cotton embroidery threads as specified on the colour key**
- **3¾mm (No 9/US 4) knitting needles**
- **Tapestry needle size 24 or 26**

To make up the cushion:
- **3¼mm (No 10/US 3) knitting needles**
- **4 buttons**
- **41cm (16in) square cushion pad**
- **Basic sewing kit**

TO KNIT THE CUSHION FRONT

Using 3¾mm (No 9/US 4) knitting needles and yellow DK yarn, cast on 96 stitches and work 1 row knit (K), 1 row purl (P) before starting the pattern. Working in stocking stitch (1 row K, 1 row P), work 2 full repeats of the pattern, and then a part repeat up to the 'end' line marked on the chart. Using yellow yarn, work 1 row K and 1 row P, then cast off. This makes a total of 110 rows.

TO WORK THE EMBROIDERY

Cross stitch is worked on knitting in the same way as it is on woven fabrics, working one cross stitch over one knitted stitch. Stitch firmly, but not so tightly as to distort the knitting. Work the watermelon design centrally in the yellow stripe, following the chart, then leave a gap of 9 stitches on either side and stitch 2 more motifs. Repeat this in the second stripe.

Working cross stitch on knitting

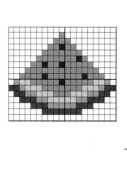

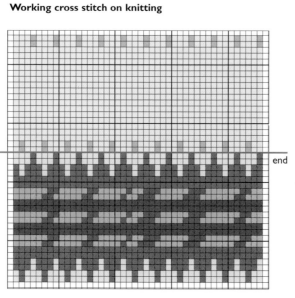

end

Anchor	DMC	skeins
210	562	1
240	955	1
259	772	1
1023	3712	2
897	221	1

	yarn colour	50g balls
	yellow	1
	bright blue	2
	light blue	1
	raspberry	1
	pink	1
	turquoise	1

TO MAKE UP THE CUSHION

To make the back of the cushion, using 3¾mm (No 9/US 4) knitting needles and working in stocking stitch, knit 2 pieces in bright blue DK yarn, each 45 stitches by 110 rows.

Using 3¼mm (No 10/US 3) knitting needles and light blue knitting yarn, on one of the pieces pick up one stitch into the end of each row to make a total of 110 stitches, then work 3 rows of K1 P1 rib. To create the buttonholes on the next row, work 21 stitches of rib, bring the yarn forward and K 2 together, work 20 stitches of rib, bring the yarn forward and K 2 together, work 20 stitches of rib, bring the yarn forward and K 2 together, work 20 stitches of rib, bring the yarn forward and K 2 together, then work 21 stitches of rib. Work 3 rows of rib, then cast off in rib.

On the other piece, pick up a stitch into the end of each row to make a total of 110 stitches and work 7 rows of K1 P1 rib, then cast off in rib. Overlapping the ribbed edges and with right sides facing, use light blue yarn to oversew the cushion front to the 2 cushion back pieces, then turn the cover through. Using DK yarn and following the instructions on page 108, make 10 tassels, each 8cm (3⅛in) long (2 in pink, 2 in turquoise, 2 in yellow, 2 in raspberry and 2 in light blue). Stitch them into the seam along the ends of the cushion cover. Stitch the buttons in place, lining them up with the buttonholes, then insert the cushion pad and button up the cover.

variations

If you are not a confident enough knitter to tackle the jacquard design, replace it with a simple stripe using the same colours, or find a fabric with a stripe or check big enough to accommodate the watermelon motif (3.5cm/1⅜in deep embroidered through 11 count waste canvas or 2.5cm/1in through 14 count). The watermelon has been embroidered through 11 count waste canvas on to a brightly coloured, woven madras check napkin that is perfect for alfresco dining.

citrus

Cushions in orange, lemon or lime are the perfect way to add a dash of fashionable citrus colour to seating, inside or out. These cushions combine raw silks in blocks of strong colour, incorporating dark green and white for their calming influence. Fruity cross-sections are featured on the buttons, which show the wonderful star shape formed by the segments.

Citrus belong to the Rutaceae family and are some of the very few trees in this group of plants, which also includes the strong-smelling herb rue. Originally from China and southeast Asia, citrus fruits came to the Mediterranean countries via India and Arabia. They were highly prized because of their rarity, as they could not be grown outdoors in cooler climates, which led to the building of orangeries in the gardens of many of the great houses in Europe in the 17th century. The fruits develop from small, white star-shaped flowers and take up to a year to ripen.

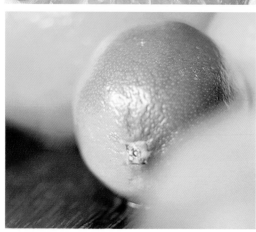

Skill level: INTERMEDIATE

The finished cushion measures 35 x 55cm (13¾ x 21⅝in), and incorporates 6 embroidered buttons.

MATERIALS
To embroider the design:
- **Scraps of 14 count waste canvas**
- **6 pieces of contrast silk fabric, each 8 x 8cm (3⅛ x 3⅛in), for the buttons**
- **Stranded cotton embroidery threads as specified on the colour key**
- **Tapestry needle size 24 or 26**

To make up the cushion:
- **2 pieces of contrast silk fabric, each 38 x 28cm (15 x 11in)**
- **Piece of main silk fabric, 38 x 38cm (15 x 15in), for the cushion back**
- **Piece of main silk fabric, 38 x 52cm (15 x 20½in), for the cushion front**
- **6 29mm (1¼in) easy-cover buttons**
- **35 x 55cm (13¾ x 21⅝in) cushion pad**
- **Basic sewing kit**

TO WORK THE EMBROIDERY

Cut out 6 pieces of 14 count waste canvas, each 18 x 18 squares, and tack a piece in position at the centre of each of the contrast fabric squares to be used for the buttons. Work the design on the fabric through the waste canvas (see page 97 for details on working with waste canvas). Strip out the waste canvas, trim each of the fabric squares into a circle 5cm (2in) in diameter and make up the buttons following the instructions supplied with the button-covering kit.

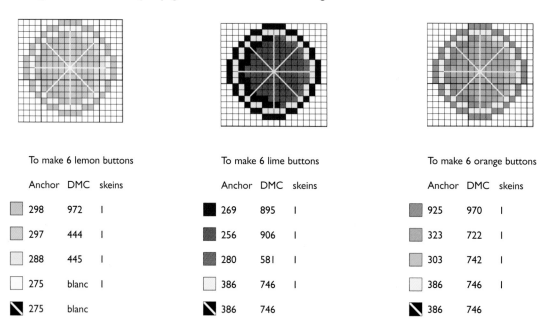

To make 6 lemon buttons

	Anchor	DMC	skeins
■	298	972	I
■	297	444	I
■	288	445	I
☐	275	blanc	I
◼	275	blanc	

To make 6 lime buttons

	Anchor	DMC	skeins
■	269	895	I
■	256	906	I
■	280	581	I
☐	386	746	I
◼	386	746	

To make 6 orange buttons

	Anchor	DMC	skeins
■	925	970	I
■	323	722	I
■	303	742	I
☐	386	746	I
◼	386	746	

TO MAKE UP THE CUSHION

Pin, tack and sew the 2 pieces of contrast fabric to the cushion back and press the seam open. Neaten the remaining raw edges of the contrast fabric and the 2 shorter edges of the cushion front. With the back section wrong side up, fold the contrast fabric over so that the wrong sides are together and press in a crease 10cm (4in) from the seam, then another 10cm (4in) from the last with right sides together. Do this at both ends, then with the cushion back right side up and the cushion front on top, right side down, fold, pin, tack and stitch them together, 2.5cm (⅝in) from the edge along the 2 long sides. Trim the corners across diagonally and turn the cover through. Work 3 equally spaced buttonholes at the openings on both ends, 1cm (⅜in) from the edge (see page 104). When the cover is complete, insert the cushion pad and button up the cover.

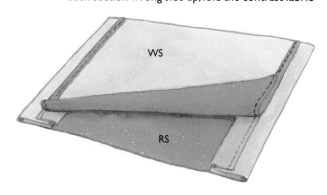

Assembling the cushion cover

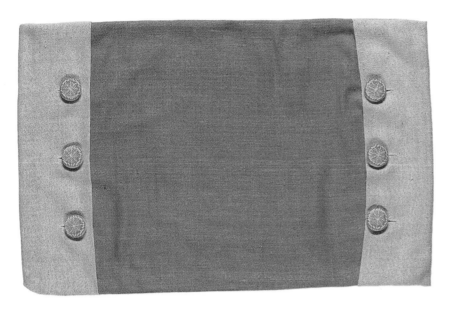

variations

These buttons can be used on many different styles of cushion cover. Use them decoratively in combination with a simple patchwork or checked fabric in citrus colours. A single button at the centre of an envelope cushion would also have real impact. Enliven storage by embroidering the design around the lid of a covered box. Draw on to your fabric around the lid of the box that is to be covered and extend the lines at the corners by the height of the lid plus 2.5cm (1in). Cut out a square of fabric at each corner, leaving a 1.5cm (⅝in) seam allowance (1). Stitch the corner seams with right sides together and press them open. Work the embroidery through waste canvas, then glue the cover to the lid with fabric adhesive, turning the extra fabric to the inside for a neat finish (2). Repeat the process to cover the bottom of the box, leaving it unembroidered.

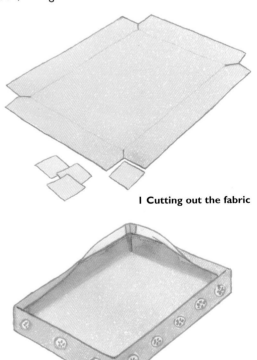

1 Cutting out the fabric

2 Covering the box lid

trailing nasturtiums

This bright little cushion is filled to overflowing with glowing orange nasturtiums. The vivid trumpet-shaped flowers are set among circular leaves with their distinctive starburst veining. Boldly contrasting turquoise borders provide the formal structure through which the plant scrambles.

Brought to Europe from Peru in the 16th century, the nasturtium has now established itself as a cottage garden favourite because of its twining, abundant habit. It is particularly welcome towards the end of the summer as it extends the season by continuing to flower until the first frost. The nasturtium is also known as Indian cress because both flowers and leaves can be eaten, adding a pleasant peppery taste and glorious colour to salads.

Skill level: EASY

Worked on 11 count Aida, the finished cushion measures 30 x 30cm (12 x 12in). Use 3 strands of cotton in the needle throughout.

MATERIALS
To embroider the design:
- **Piece of 11 count white Aida, 33 x 33cm (13 x 13in), for the cushion front**
- **Stranded cotton embroidery threads as specified in the colour key**
- **Tapestry needle size 24 or 26**

To make up the cushion:
- **2 pieces of turquoise cotton fabric, each 33 x 24cm (13 x 9½in), for the cushion back**
- **125cm (50in) length of piping cord, covered with turquoise fabric**
- **3 buttons**
- **30cm (12in) square cushion pad**
- **Basic sewing kit**

TO WORK THE EMBROIDERY

Start stitching at one of the corners, 11 squares in from both the horizontal and vertical edges of the fabric (the design itself measures 28 x 28 cm/11 x 11 in). Establishing the outer edge of the border first provides some good reference points for placing the rest of the design.

TO MAKE UP THE CUSHION

The cushion is finished with a piped edge and a button back (see pages 106 and 104). When the cover is complete, insert the cushion pad and button up the cover.

variations

Make the kitchen a cosier place by softening wooden chairs with squab cushions, held in place with fabric ties and embroidered with clusters of nasturtiums. A table runner is a traditional piece of household linen with which to dress a table. Combining the nasturtium flower with a check emphasizes the country feel of the design and the check becomes the framework for the plant to scramble through.

	Anchor	DMC	skeins
	351	400	1
	326	720	2
	1002	976	1
	1066	3808	3
	212	561	1
	244	701	3
	241	703	2
	255	471	1

the pale room

Whether they are fresh and clean or sunbleached and worn, pale colours are always calming and easy to live with. Summer will never feel far away when you are surrounded by the light, airy atmosphere that these colours can create.

Bringing together white with just one other colour has purity, the impact is instant and undiluted. Furnishings and accessories in different textures and tones of the chosen colour will add a subtlety of contrast and depth to the scheme. Blue and white is a classic and harmonious two-colour combination, familiar because of the enduring popularity of Chinese porcelain and Delft tiles. Chalky grey-blues in combination with antique white are reminiscent of the Gustavian era of 18th-century Sweden, especially where the scheme incorporates matt textures and signs of faded grandeur. The slightly warmer lavender and white, with its pink undertone, is a more contemporary combination, which is both homely and sophisticated. Pale colours also combine well with each other, and, more so than with any other group, schemes using four or five colours in equal proportions can be very successful.

pale

White or neutral walls act as a backdrop against which furnishings in soft colours can be set without being overpowered. Add one wall in a pastel shade to create a focal point within the room, or paint each wall a different colour for a contemporary look. Colours containing the same proportion of white are said to be of the same tone. Because they are equally prominent, these colours will not fight each other and combine well in colourblocking. Colourwashed walls have a rough, chalky look, easily created by brushing thinned emulsion over a base coat of a similar colour. The resulting random mixing of tones is particularly good on irregular surfaces. Tinted oil-based glazes applied over an eggshell base give a similar effect, creating pale colour that has great depth and texture but with a translucent finish and subtle sheen. Painted tongue-and-groove panelling can inspire a relaxed beach-hut style, while covering uneven walls and providing added insulation.

Plain pale colours, particularly blue and green, are a good choice for small spaces that need brightening up. They reflect light, receding to enhance the feeling of space. Floaty, sheer fabrics draped at the window cast a diffuse, filtered light that is gentle on the eyes while providing privacy from the world outside. A piece of antique lace creates a dappled light and introduces a touch of old-fashioned charm.

Where walls and furniture are pale in colour, a dark floor could easily appear very heavy. Simple cleaning and sanding can lighten the colour of a wooden

floor to dramatic effect. Hardwood floors can be treated with lime in order to bring out the pattern of the grain and lighten the colour. Where floorboards are in very bad condition or floors are made from concrete or chipboard, they can be painted.

Open and transparent materials, such as frosted glass, brushed aluminium, metallic mesh or fretworked wood, can be used to make shelving and cupboard fronts for storage and display. Pale colours diluted with light have a shimmering, iridescent quality, quite different from that produced by adding white pigment to paint. Collections of glassware in the translucent colours of amethyst, aquamarine and other semi-precious stones look magical with sunlight streaming through them. Mother-of-pearl encrusted boxes and china with opalescent glazes display the lustrous beauty of light itself. Reflect or counterbalance the mood of a room with your choice of flowers and the way in which they are displayed. Delicate sweet peas positioned casually on a windowsill look at home in a relaxed room with a nostalgic atmosphere, while a vase of silvery blue-green eucalyptus pulls the pale room away from unashamed femininity.

To be practical, everyday soft furnishings in pale colours should have removable covers and be machine washable, or they will soon lose the freshness of their colour. Otherwise, reserve pale colours for rooms where they can be taken care of, such as a formal drawing room or an adult's bedroom. Pale colours show up the texture of stitching or pattern woven into a fabric. Sheer and fleecy fabrics also make the best of pale colours. In winter, luxurious layers of blankets, throws and cushions in knitted, brushed and pile fabrics soften the edges of a pale room, turning it into a winter wonderland.

The embroidery designs for the pale room reflect the wide range of style directions that can be taken in this colour group: from Modesty to Heartsease, from the sublime to the flirty!

Bringing together white with just one other colour has purity, the impact is instant and undiluted. Furnishings and accessories in different textures and tones of the chosen colour will add a subtlety of contrast and depth to the scheme.

modesty

The features of this statue have been broken down into an intriguing pattern of light and shade, creating a subtle mix of colour and texture when worked in antique white thread against a muted violet background. Tassels add a touch of whimsy, held in place at each corner by an embroidered claw.

The pure, uncomplicated lines of a bust, statuette or urn in cool white marble have restrained elegance and conjure up a romanticized vision of the classical styles of Ancient Greece and Rome. This design was inspired by a 17th-century bust, whose sideways glance is full of humility and propriety, earning her the name Modesty.

Skill level: INTERMEDIATE

Worked on 28 count evenweave fabric, the finished cushion measures 46 x 46cm (18 x 18in). Use 2 strands of cotton in the needle throughout, working each stitch over 2 fabric threads to give 14 stitches per 2.5cm (1in).

MATERIALS
To embroider the design:
• **Piece of 28 count light violet cotton-mix evenweave fabric, 49 x 49cm (19¼ x 19¼in) for the cushion front**
• **Stranded cotton embroidery threads as specified in the colour key**
• **Tapestry needle size 24 or 26**

To make up the cushion:
• **2 pieces of 28 count light violet evenweave fabric, each 49 x 26cm (19¼ x 10¼in) for the cushion back**
• **30cm (12in) violet zip**
• **3 skeins of stranded cotton embroidery thread (Anchor 926/DMC ecru), for the tassels**
• **46cm (18in) square cushion pad**
• **Basic sewing kit**

<table>
<tr><td>

**TO WORK THE
EMBROIDERY**

</td><td>

Using running stitch, mark the position of all 4 corners of the finished cushion. Mark the first corner 1.5cm (⅝in) in from both the horizontal and vertical edges of the fabric. Measure 46cm (18in) along to the second corner and mark it roughly with a pin, then follow the thread of the fabric between the 2 corners to ensure that the second falls exactly in line with the first. The third corner can be marked in the same way; the fourth corner is found by following the fabric thread from the first and third corners to the point where they meet.

Begin by stitching the 'claw' designs up to each of the 4 corner markers, following the chart. Position the face centrally between the corners by matching the central points on the chart to the central points on the fabric (see page 99), then work the image following the chart. When stitching over large areas in a single colour it is particularly important to prepare the thread properly, separating and re-combining the strands, to achieve a uniform stitch (see page 98).

</td></tr>
</table>

<table>
<tr><td>

**TO MAKE UP THE
CUSHION**

</td><td>

The cushion is finished with a plain seamed edge, a zip fastening and a hand-made tassel at each corner (see pages 105, 102 and 108). When the cover is complete, insert the cushion pad and close the zip.

</td></tr>
</table>

variations

The clasp and tassel corner detail would make plain cushions in luxurious fabrics such as figured velvets and silk brocades even more splendid, particularly if a metallic blending filament were incorporated into the stitching. The design adorns the corners of this crisp white damask tablecloth in stitches of the palest blue-grey, creating an understatedly elegant table. It was worked with 2 strands of cotton in the needle, through 14 count waste canvas.

147

↑104

Anchor DMC skeins

◥ 926   ecru   5

heartsease

This design takes a formal approach to florals, with the repetition of a flowerhead within a framework, while diaphanous voiles in pale colours soften the effect. Like a series of framed portraits, each flower is given an individual expression by the variation in their colour markings.

Heartsease is traditionally associated with love, and many of its common names reflect this. Referred to in *A Midsummer Night's Dream* as love-in-idleness, Oberon squeezes the juice of the heartsease on Titania's eyelids as she sleeps, so that she will fall in love. Because of its tricoloured flowers of cream, yellow and purple, it is also sometimes called herb trinity.

Skill level: INTERMEDIATE

With the appliqué squares worked on 14 count Aida, giving 14 stitches per 2.5cm (1in), the finished cushion measures 46 x 46cm (18 x 18in), plus a 3cm (1¼in) Oxford border. Use 2 strands of cotton in the needle throughout.

MATERIALS
To embroider the design:
- **9 pieces of 14 count white Aida, each 10 x 10cm (4 x 4in)**
- **2 blue, 2 yellow, 2 green and 3 lavender pieces of voile, each 10 x 10cm (4 x 4in)**
- **Stranded cotton embroidery threads as specified in the colour key**
- **Tapestry needle size 24 or 26**

To make up the cushion:
- **Piece of linen fabric, 55 x 55cm (21⅝ x 21⅝in), for the cushion front**
- **2 pieces of linen fabric, each 55 x 35cm (21⅝ x 13¾in), for the cushion back**
- **Sewing threads matched to the voile colours**
- **3 buttons**
- **46cm (18in) square cushion pad**
- **Basic sewing kit**

TO WORK THE
EMBROIDERY

Prepare all 9 squares for embroidery in advance,
tacking the voile on top of the Aida squares, with
the right side of both fabrics facing upwards. Work
a different flowerhead in the centre of each square.
Use the Aida behind the voile to count and space
the stitches while stitching through both layers of
fabric. When all 9 squares are complete, trim them
down to 8 x 8cm (3⅛ x 3⅛in).

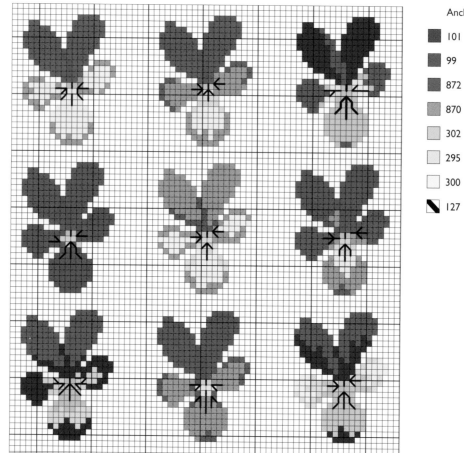

Anchor	DMC	skeins
101	550	1
99	552	1
872	3041	1
870	3042	1
302	743	1
295	726	1
300	3823	1
127	823	1

TO MAKE UP THE CUSHION

Place the squares on the cushion front with a 2cm (¾in) gap between each square. Tack the squares in position and then sew around them with a close zigzag stitch, using a thread colour-matched to the voile in that particular square. To create neat corners, sew a distance the width of the zigzag stitch beyond the end of the square, and with the needle in the fabric and in the outer side of the stitch, lift the foot and turn the fabric through 90 degrees, then lower the foot and continue stitching.

The cushion is finished with an Oxford or single flange border and a button back (see pages 106 and 104). When the cover is complete, insert the cushion pad and button up the cover.

variations

A simple patchwork cushion cover in squares of cream, yellow and purple would be transformed by embroidering a heartsease on some or all of the squares. Sheer curtains let in a tempered light, filtered and coloured by translucent fabric. This border of appliquéd flowerheads adds a decorative touch and casts pretty squares of shadow when the sun shines. To achieve layers of transparency, the squares were worked on the same sheer muslin as the curtain, using 14 count waste canvas, then appliquéd in place.

feathers

This design captures some of the lightness and delicacy of a feather. The simplicity of a two-colour design emphasizes details in shape, like the curve of its quill and the downiness at its base. Blue promotes tranquillity, particularly soft blue-grey, which is both elegant and restful. This cushion has a formalized border design of feather-like shapes surrounding naturalistic images of feathers meandering through space. Their airy softness makes them a very comfortable image upon which to relax.

Feathers form a mesh of interlinked filaments over which air will flow, enabling birds to fly. They differ greatly in size and shape. Tail and wing feathers tend to be large and smooth, while those from the body tend to be smaller and downy.

Skill level: INTERMEDIATE

Worked on 28 count evenweave fabric, the finished cushion measures 44 x 26cm (17¼ x 10¼in), plus a 3cm (1⅛in) Oxford border. Use 2 strands of cotton in the needle throughout, working each stitch over 2 fabric threads to give 14 stitches per 2.5cm (1in).

MATERIALS
To embroider the design:
- **Piece of 28 count blue-grey cotton-mix evenweave fabric, 53 x 35cm (20⅞ x 13¾in), for the cushion front**
- **Stranded cotton embroidery thread as specified in the colour key**
- **Tapestry needle size 24 or 26**

To make up the cushion:
- **2 pieces of blue-grey cotton-mix evenweave fabric, each 34 x 35cm (13⅜ x 13¾in), for the cushion back**
- **Piece of blue-grey cotton-mix evenweave fabric, 8 x 8cm (3⅛ x 3⅛in), for the button**
- **29mm (1¼in) easy-cover button**
- **44 x 26cm (17¼ x 10¼in) cushion pad**
- **Basic sewing kit**

TO WORK THE EMBROIDERY

Begin stitching the border (see chart on page 90), starting with a corner motif 4cm (1½in) in from both the horizontal and vertical edges of the fabric. Work the design by repeating the sections as shown on the chart.

The positioning of the central feathers need not be exact and every cushion will be a little bit different. Placing is done by eye, referring to the border design in combination with the picture opposite. Using the maximum height and width of each feather as a guide, mark on the fabric the blocks within which each feather is worked, in running stitch.

Alternatively, you may feel confident enough to stitch without markers. Start from a key spot on the feather, like the end of the quill, checking its positioning in relation to the border both horizontally and vertically. Once the first couple of stitches are established in the right place, follow the chart as usual.

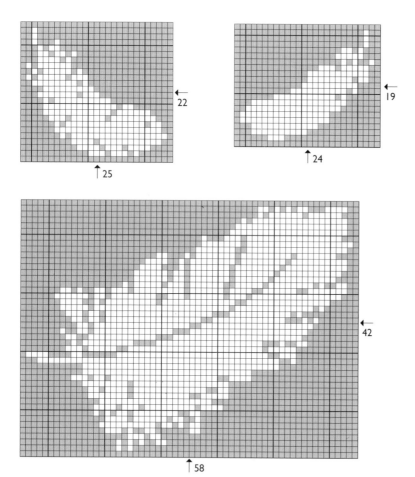

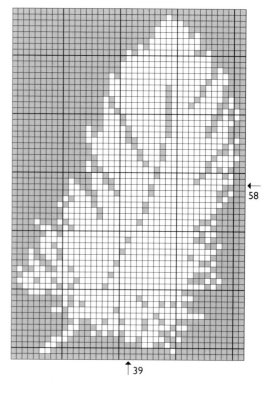

Anchor	DMC	skeins
1037	3756	4

TO MAKE UP THE CUSHION

The feathers cushion is finished with an Oxford, or single flange, border and a button back (see pages 106 and 104). Embroider the single button with a star design following the chart opposite, then make it up following the instructions which are supplied with the button-covering kit. When the cover is complete, insert the cushion pad and button up the cover.

88

↑ 47

↓ 15

→ 15

variations

This cushion would look frivolously pretty with the feathers stitched in palest pink, lavender and sky blue on a white fabric background. Because feathers were used as early writing implements, a single feather would look appropriate embroidered on a fabric sleeve for a notebook. Plain and checked cotton chambrays are a classic combination for this comforting baby's cot quilt. The border design defines an area that has been quilted using a simple, old-fashioned method known as tufting. A series of stitches is passed twice through all the layers of the quilt, then tied in a double knot on the front of the quilt and the ends neatly trimmed.

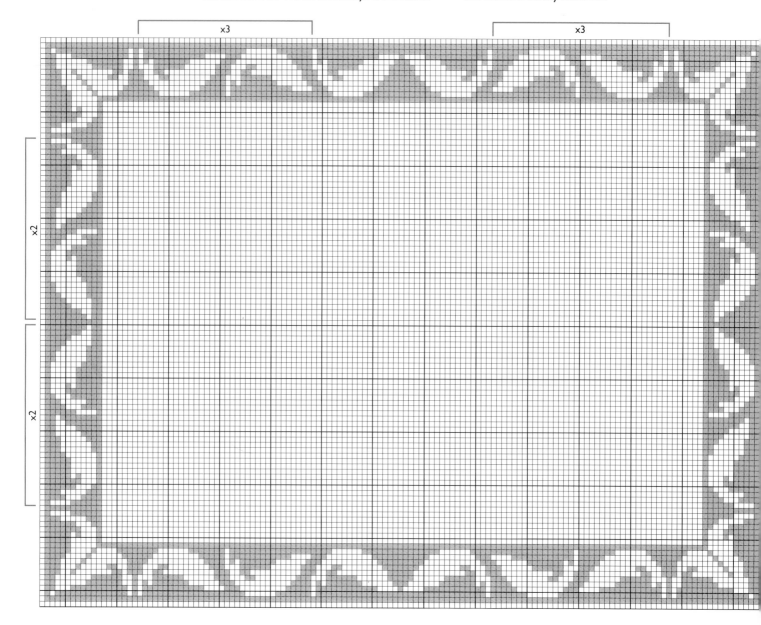

clover

Embroidered borders of clover against a white cotton background make a charming and useful little cushion. The character of this humble but pretty weed is captured in the large stitches and simple colouring of the design. The cushion is finished with antique lace and closed at the back with tied cotton tapes, adding to the homely, unaffected look.

Fragrant wild clover (*Trifolium pratense*) grows in abundance in meadows, pastures and on roadsides. The sweetly scented flowerheads held on long, thin stems are irresistible to bees, which collect nectar and turn it into delicious honey. Living a comfortable, fortunate life is often expressed as 'living in clover' because of the contentment of cattle put to graze in clover-rich pastures, and everyone knows that finding a four-leaved clover brings good luck.

Skill level: EASY

Worked on 28 count evenweave fabric, the finished cushion measures 41 x 30cm (16 x 12in). Use 3 strands of cotton in the needle throughout, working each stitch over 3 fabric threads to give approximately 9½ stitches per 2.5cm (1in).

MATERIALS

To embroider the design:
- **Piece of 28 count white cotton-mix evenweave fabric, 44 x 33cm (17¼ x 13in), for the cushion front**
- **Stranded cotton embroidery threads as specified in the colour key**
- **Tapestry needle size 24 or 26**

To make up the cushion:
- **2 pieces of white cotton-mix evenweave fabric, each 44 x 18cm (17¼ x 7in), for the cushion back**
- **2 pieces of white cotton-mix evenweave fabric, each 44 x 10cm (17¼ x 4in), for the facings**
- **130cm (51in) length of antique white lace**
- **2 30cm (12in) lengths of antique white tape**
- **41 x 30cm (16 x 12in) cushion pad**
- **Basic sewing kit**

TO WORK THE EMBROIDERY

Start 1.5cm (⅝in) in from the horizontal and vertical edges of the fabric to allow for the seams. Work the design along one of the long edges of the fabric, repeating it continuously 4 times, to end up 1.5cm (⅝in) in from the other side. Turn the fabric around and repeat the whole process along the opposite edge.

	Anchor	DMC	skeins
	215	320	4
	260	3348	3
	292	3078	1
	1016	3727	1

TO MAKE UP THE CUSHION

The cushion is finished with antique lace across each end and an informal tie fastening on the back (see pages 107 and 105). When the cover is complete, insert the cushion pad and tie the back closed.

variations

Sprigs of clover embroidered here and there on a gingham fabric temper its utilitarian simplicity with a touch of delicacy and would be suitable for a cushion cover, tablecloth, quilt or drawstring bag. Plain cotton blinds are softened by a small embroidered detail above the pull. The section of the design was chosen to form a triangular outline rather than using a straight repeat. It was embroidered with 3 strands of cotton through 11 count waste canvas.

materials, equipment and techniques

This chapter covers everything you need to know to embroider the designs in this book and to achieve a professional-looking finish to the cushions. The techniques involved are all very straightforward, and you may well already be familiar with many of them.

MATERIALS AND EQUIPMENT
FABRICS FOR CROSS STITCH

Most cross stitch projects are worked on fabric that has an even weave and threads that are pronounced enough to be counted by eye. The fabric used is woven with the same number of threads over a given length both horizontally and vertically so that the shapes of motifs embroidered on it are not distorted.

blockweave fabric (Aida)

Aida is an excellent fabric for beginners. Its weave forms distinct blocks that are easy to count, and the blocks relate directly to the squares on the chart. Between the blocks are large, clearly defined holes for the needle to pass through, which makes it easy to stitch.

Some of the projects in this book use 11 and 14 count Aida fabrics, which means that they have 11 or 14 squares per 2.5cm (1in). The higher the count of the fabric, the finer it will be, so 14 count Aida is stitched using 2 strands of cotton in the needle, while 3 strands are used to create a fuller stitch that will cover the bigger blocks of 11 count fabric.

Any of the evenweave projects in the book can be stitched on Aida in order to make them easier to tackle.

evenweave linen, cotton and cotton-mix fabrics

These fabrics are finer than Aida and have a more sophisticated appearance. They are of plain-weave construction, which is the simplest weave type. The threads are clearly defined, making the fabrics easy to stitch accurately, but they are still more challenging to work than Aida.

Evenweave fabrics are available in a range of counts. Some of the projects in this book use 27 or 28 count fabrics, which have 27 or 28 fabric threads per 2.5cm (1in) but are worked with each stitch taken over 2, or in some cases 3, fabric threads. For example, 28 count stitched over 2 threads results in 14 stitches per 2.5cm (1in) and the stitch is the same size as that made on a 14 count Aida.

Linen has a crisp handle and comes in a range of beautiful natural colours. Cotton and cotton-mix evenweaves have a softer handle, a more closed appearance and will drape well, making them suitable for tablecloths and many other household projects.

colour

Both blockweave and evenweave fabrics are available in a range of colours, but you could also consider dying and fabric painting to achieve unusual shades. Cold-water dye is suitable for imparting colour to a small quantity of fabric and disturbs the spacing of the fabric threads least. The colour becomes permanent with the addition of a fixative. With cotton Aida and cotton-mix evenweave fabrics, the resulting colour will be paler than with pure cotton and linen evenweaves. Fabric paints also produce good results, particularly on evenweave linen, and are excellent for very small projects or for creating multicoloured backgrounds. Always follow the instructions supplied with the particular paint or dye you are using.

waste canvas

Waste canvas makes it possible to stitch on almost any fabric, even if it is not possible to count the threads or if the threads are uneven. The texture of the stitching contrasts beautifully with finely woven cotton, chiffon or chenille backgrounds, adding another dimension to the design.

Waste canvas provides a grid that can be sewn through to create stitches that are even in size and spacing. The canvas is held together with starch and is easily stripped out from under the completed stitching. Coloured guidelines are woven into the canvas to aid in its orientation and the counting of its squares. Some of the projects in this book use 11 and 14 count waste canvas, resulting in stitches equivalent in size to 11 and 14 count Aida.

When using waste canvas, begin by counting the number of squares on the chart over which the design is worked and cut a piece of waste canvas that is at least 2 squares bigger all round. If the motif is placed centrally, fold both the canvas and the fabric in half, and then in half again, to locate the central point on both. Lay the canvas on top of the fabric with the central points lined up, ensuring that the coloured guidelines on the canvas are aligned with the grain of the fabric. Pin and tack the canvas in place on the background fabric. If the motif is large you may wish to mark a central line horizontally and vertically on the chart with a pencil and on the canvas with a running stitch, which can be stitched over but then removed on

completion. Smaller designs worked through waste canvas can be mounted in an embroidery hoop if you wish, but I would not recommend trapping the waste canvas itself between the 2 hoops as this might distort the canvas and lead to uneven stitching.

Begin stitching the design at a point that is easily identifiable on both the canvas and the chart. Work through the centre of each hole in the canvas and pass the needle through both the canvas and the fabric. Where stitches meet they should share the same point of insertion in the fabric, to prevent messy gaps between the stitches.

When the cross stitching is complete, remove the tacking and running-stitch markers and trim off any large areas of excess canvas to within 1cm (⅜in) of the stitching. It is sometimes advised that you dampen the waste canvas before removing it, but this can leave a sticky residue so I recommend that you leave it dry. Use a blunt-ended needle and tweezers to withdraw the threads of the canvas, one at a time, beginning with the vertical ones. The horizontal threads will then be free and can be gently eased out. Backstitch detail is added after the waste canvas has been withdrawn.

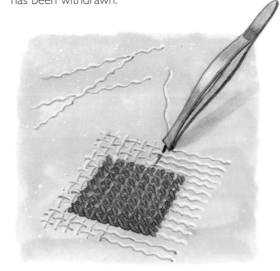

Removing waste canvas once the stitching has been completed

EMBROIDERY NEEDLES

A size 24 or 26 blunt-ended tapestry needle is recommended for stitching the projects in this book. The size 26 needle is slightly finer and therefore more suitable for stitching on finer fabrics, while the size 24 needle has a slightly larger eye, which is easier to thread, especially when using 3 strands of cotton. A tapestry needle has a rounded point that slides between the fabric threads rather than splitting them, and quite a large eye, which makes threading multiple strands of cotton easier.

Each type of thread has a different degree of elasticity. When different threads are mixed in the same needle, as when a metallic blending filament is included with stranded cotton, it is a good idea to knot the blending filament on to the needle.

Loop the thread and pass the loop through the eye of the needle (1). Put the thread over the end of the needle (2) and tighten the loop at the end of the eye (3), gently stroking the knotted thread to 'lock' it in place (4).

EMBROIDERY THREADS

Six-stranded embroidery cotton is the thread most commonly used for cross stitch. It is available in a good range of colours, has a nice uniform lustre and is colourfast. Cut the thread into manageable lengths of about 46cm (18in). Separate each strand and then re-combine the number of strands appropriate to the fabric count. This prevents the strands twisting around each other and gives better cover and a smoother appearance to the stitch.

STITCHING THE DESIGN
PREPARING THE FABRIC

Cut the fabric to the required size and zigzag stitch, oversew or bind the edges with masking tape to prevent them from fraying while the fabric is being worked.

Mark out the position of the motif or motifs with running stitch in a contrast thread. If the motif is positioned centrally, fold the fabric in half horizontally and run tacking stitches along the fold. Repeat the process vertically; where the 2 lines of stitching cross is the centre of the fabric. The arrows that are shown on the chart indicate the centre points of the design and correspond with the tacked lines.

Some people prefer to work with the fabric in their hands while others like to use a hoop or frame to help achieve a more even stitch. Hoops come in a range of sizes and are ideal for smaller motifs or they can be moved around the fabric for larger designs. Binding the inner rim with cotton tape gives it a better grip and prevents marking of

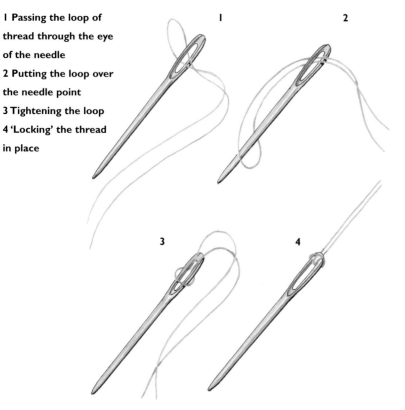

1 Passing the loop of thread through the eye of the needle

2 Putting the loop over the needle point

3 Tightening the loop

4 'Locking' the thread in place

the fabric. Remove the outer ring and place the fabric over the bound inner ring, making sure that the design is centred in the hoop. Replace the outer ring and tighten the screw until the fabric is pulled taut. Remove or loosen the hoop at the end of each stitching session to avoid any permanent distortion of the fabric.

A slate frame is ideal for larger projects. The top and bottom edges of the fabric are wound around rollers to keep it under tension and hold the threads of the fabric square. Frames can be hand-held or free-standing. In the latter case both hands are free, and with one hand above and one below the fabric the stitching process is greatly speeded up.

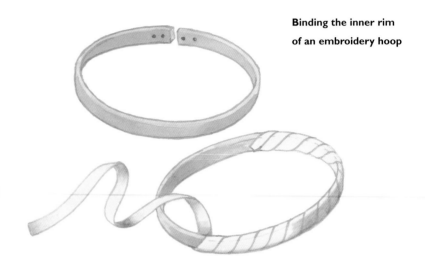

Binding the inner rim of an embroidery hoop

READING THE CHARTS

The charts in this book show the stitches as coloured blocks against a background grid, each square of the grid representing one stitch. Count the number of blocks on the chart and work the same number of stitches in the given colour of thread. Backstitch is denoted by a line in the appropriate colour.

The key lists the code number of each thread used against the colour as it appears on the chart. These colours have been matched as closely as possible to the thread colour without compromising the chart's clarity. The key gives the colour code numbers in both Anchor and DMC systems. The designs have been stitched with Anchor threads and these have been translated to the nearest DMC thread colour for your convenience, but if you use DMC threads your work may not match the photographed pieces exactly. The key also shows the number of skeins of each colour required to complete the design.

The centre points, both horizontal and vertical, have been marked on some of the charts, along with the number of stitches that the design covers in each direction. This is to help you in positioning

the design or elements of it on the fabric. If you colour photocopy the chart you wish to use, enlarge it to make counting easier and mark the chart with additional reference lines and notes.

Anchor	DMC	skeins
1007	3772	1

A back stitch key

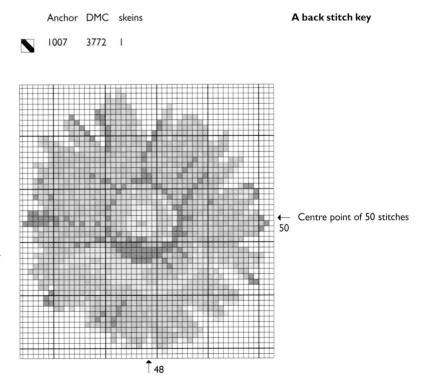

← Centre point of 50 stitches
50

↑ 48

1 Making the first diagonal of a single cross stitch

2 Completing a single cross stitch

3 Working a row of cross stitches

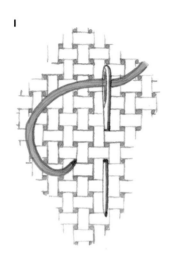

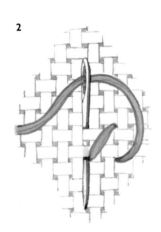

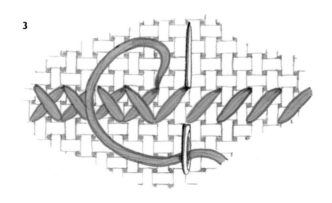

STITCH TECHNIQUES
cross stitch

Thread the needle with the appropriate number of strands in the required thread colour. Push the needle up through the fabric where the first stitch is to be made. Hold a short length of thread on the underside of the work and catch it in the back of the first few stitches to secure it. Never knot the end as this will make the work lumpy and in time the knot can work its way through to the front.

Complete one area of colour at a time and avoid carrying threads over more than a few stitches. Although I am not one of those who judge the quality of a piece of cross stitching by the neatness of the back, keeping it in reasonable order prevents frustrating tangles and knots forming.

The stitches must all cross in the same direction to create a uniform, evenly textured surface. Depending on personal preference and the nature of the design, stitches can be completed individually or in horizontal or vertical rows. To make a single stitch, bring the needle up through the fabric to the front at the bottom left. Insert it one block up and to the right, bring it out one block below (1), then insert it one block up to the left to complete the cross (2).

To make a row of diagonal stitches, work from right to left and from top right to bottom left of the stitch. When you have worked the required number of stitches, work back along the row from left to right, crossing the stitches already worked, from top left to bottom right (3). This is the fastest technique when stitching large blocks of stitches in one colour, but take care to keep an even tension.

You can work in any direction and combine single stitches with rows, as long as the top thread always crosses in the same direction.

To finish off neatly, pass the needle through to the back of the fabric and through the back of the last few stitches. Cut off the end of the thread to prevent it catching in subsequent stitches.

backstitch

Backstitch is used to add fine lines and detail to a design. It should be added after all the cross stitching has been completed. The number of strands of cotton to use is given in the instructions for each design.

Bring the needle up through the fabric, the length of one stitch ahead of the start of the line to be sewn. Take it back down through to the reverse of the fabric at the start of the line. Bring it up through the fabric again, the length of one stitch ahead of the previous stitch. Take it back down through to the reverse of the fabric, inserting the needle into the same hole as that through which the previous stitch came up. Continue this sequence in the direction which is indicated on the chart.

WASHING AND PRESSING

If necessary, wash the embroidered piece carefully by hand in lukewarm water and mild soap with no detergent. Even if it does not need washing, it will probably need pressing, particularly if an embroidery hoop has been used. Lay the embroidered fabric face down on a folded towel, cover with a damp cloth and iron gently until it is even. Do not iron the embroidery on the front, as this will flatten the stitches and the texture is an important part of the appeal of cross stitch.

MAKING UP THE CUSHIONS

The designs in this book are intended initially to be made up as cushions, with a variety of different edgings and fastenings. The techniques explained which follow will enable you to achieve a neat and professional-looking finish.

If you wish to use a different fastening from that

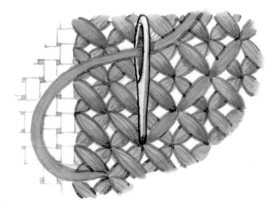

Working backstitch.

suggested in the project be sure to alter the fabric allowances for the cushion back.

SEWING EQUIPMENT

A basic sewing kit is required to make up the projects in this book. This should include dressmaking and embroidery scissors, pins and needles, a pencil, a tape measure, tailor's chalk and sewing threads in an assortment of colours. An iron and ironing board are essential for a neat finish. Although most of the projects could be completely hand stitched, a sewing machine will make the job much quicker and easier.

MEASURING AND CUTTING OUT FABRIC

Always lay out the fabric on a firm, flat surface, ensuring that there are no folds or wrinkles, and doublecheck your measurements before cutting. Use tailor's chalk to mark the position of the seamlines, zips and so on, as accuracy helps to achieve a neat finish and chalk is easily removed. Use a sharp pair of scissors to avoid damaging the fabric and cut with the whole blade by opening the scissors wide. On some fabrics it is possible to pull a fabric thread at right angles to the selvedge, which can then be followed with the scissors to help create right-angled corners.

FASTENINGS

simple openings

These openings do not produce such a professional finish as those chosen for the cushions in this book, but they are an option for those who want a simple method for making up their embroidery into a very presentable and serviceable cushion.

The simplest openings have no fastenings as such. To make a slipstitched opening, seam together 2 pieces of fabric of the same dimensions, around 3 sides and on to the fourth, then trim the seam allowance diagonally at the corners (1). Turn the cover through, insert the cushion pad, and then slipstitch the seam closed (2). With this method, removing the cover for washing is a laborious process, as the seam will have to be unpicked and then re-stitched closed, although if you do not have a sewing machine it is an option.

An envelope back is the next simplest opening. The 2 pieces of fabric that make up the cushion back should be the same width as the cushion front but half the length plus 15cm (6in). Neaten one of the edges across the width of each piece by turning under 1.5cm (⅝in). Tack the 2 back cushion pieces together, overlapping the hemmed edges by 27cm (10½in). The resulting piece should be the same size as the cushion front. Place them together with right sides facing and pin, tack and stitch 1.5cm (⅝in) from the edge, around all 4 sides. Remove the tacking, trim the seam allowance diagonally at the corners and turn the cover through, pushing out the corners.

The cushion pad can then be inserted through the opening in the back and pushed behind the overlap of fabric which keeps it in place and prevents the opening from gaping.

zip fastening

The zip is the most practical fastening for a cushion. Zips come in a variety of weights, with metal or nylon teeth attached to 2 fabric tapes. Nylon zips are available in a wider range of colours and are more flexible, which makes them the most suitable choice for a cushion. Take care when ironing as the teeth can be damaged by the heat.

The zip can be inserted in one of the seams to create a totally reversible cushion. However, as the cushions in this book have a distinct front, I prefer

1 Stitching the front and back cushion pieces together
2 Slipstitching the seam closed

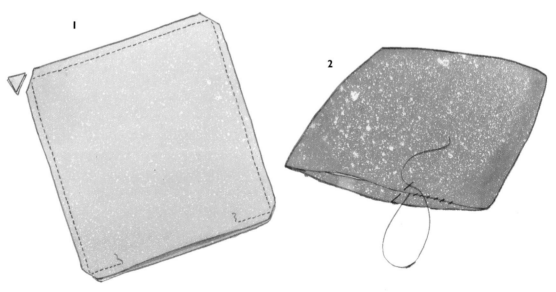

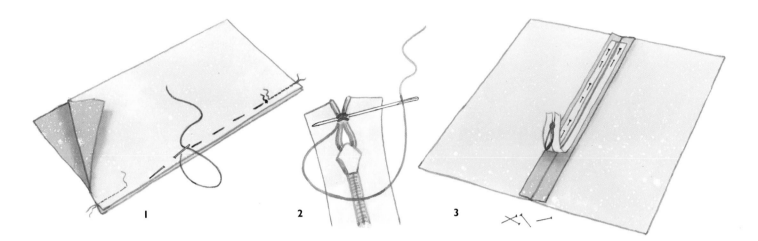

1

2

3

to put the zip in the centre of the back. Do this before attaching the back to the front, while the fabric is flat. The 2 pieces of fabric for the cushion back should be the same width as the front but half the length plus 1.5cm (⅝in) seam allowance.

Stitch the 2 back sections together at either end, leaving a gap 1cm (⅜in) longer than the length covered by the zip teeth, including the top and bottom stops. Tack the zip opening together and press the seam open (1). Stitch the zip tapes together above the top stop (2), then place the zip face down over the seam allowance, with the bottom stop 3mm (⅛in) below the beginning of the tacked section and the teeth centred exactly over the seamline. Pin and tack the zip in place down both sides, 6mm (¼in) from the teeth and stitching through all the layers (3). With the right side of the fabric facing upwards and using a zipper foot on the machine, topstitch the zip in place just inside the tacking lines. At the corners, leave the needle in the fabric, lift the foot and rotate the fabric by 90 degrees, lower the foot and continue stitching, to create a closed oblong of stitching with square corners (4). Finally, remove all the tacking, trim the seam allowance diagonally across the corners, then open the zip and turn the cover through (5).

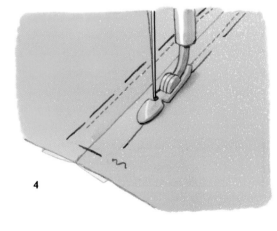

4

1 Tacking the zip opening together
2 Stitching the tapes together above the top stop
3 Tacking the zip into place
4 Topstitching the zip into place
5 Trimming the seam allowance, ready to turn the cover through

5

button fastening

Button fastenings are practical and decorative. Buttons come in an enormous range of shapes, colours and materials as well as sizes. Choose natural materials – mother-of-pearl or wood for fabrics in natural colours, and perhaps an intricate, aged metal button for a velvet. Unless specified, use buttons about 2.5cm (1in) in diameter.

To make a button fastening the 2 pieces of fabric for the cushion back should be the same width as the front and half the length plus 7.5cm (3in). Neaten one of the edges across the width of each piece by turning under 1.5 cm (⅝in). On one of the pieces, which is the side where the buttonholes will be sewn, turn under 6cm (2⅜in) and press a neat crease along the edge. Mark the seam allowance 1.5cm (⅝in) in from each edge, then space the buttonholes evenly between these points, at least 1.5cm (⅝in) from the edge (1).

To work buttonholes by hand, cut the hole first and then work buttonhole stitches as closely as possible to form a firm edging. Insert the needle upwards into the fabric and bring the point out 3mm (⅛in) from the edge. Loop the thread hanging from the eye of the needle from right to left under the point of the needle and draw the needle upwards and out of the fabric, pulling the thread tighter into a knot as it goes (2).

To machine stitch a buttonhole, use a buttonhole foot and make 2 lines of zigzag stitch with a bar at each end, before cutting down the centre to make the hole (3). Consult your machine instruction booklet for more details on sewing buttonholes using that specific machine.

With the other piece of cushion back pressed flat, overlap the 2 pieces by 6cm (2⅜in) and tack them together. Mark the position of the buttons centrally through the buttonhole on the layer underneath and stitch the buttons in place. Complete all these processes while the fabric is flat, before making up the rest of the cushion. When the cover is complete, remove the tacking, trim the seam allowance diagonally across the corners and turn the cover to the right side.

1 Positioning the buttonholes

2 Working buttonholes by hand

3 Cutting machine buttonhole after stitching

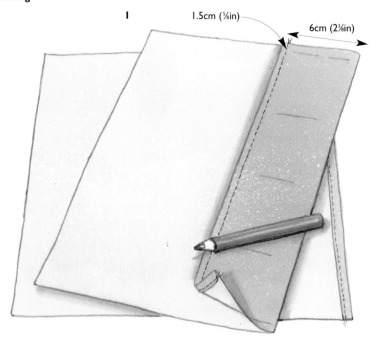

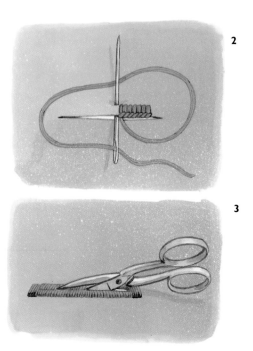

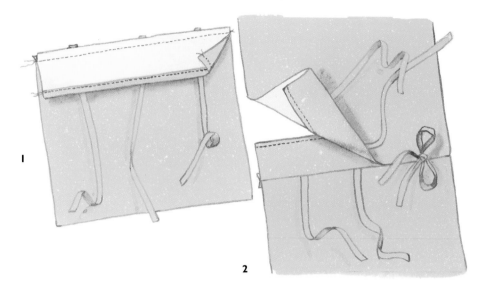

**1 Positioning and
stitching the tapes
2 Tying the tapes**

tie fastening

Fabric or ribbon ties can be used to hold together the 2 open edges of a cushion cover, giving the cushion a relaxed, informal appearance.

Cut 2 pieces of fabric for the cushion back, the same width as the front and half the length plus 1.5cm (⅝in) seam allowance. Cut 2 strips of the same fabric to form the facings. These should be equal in length to the width of the cushion back and 9cm (3½in) wide. Position 3 lengths of tape evenly across both back pieces. Lay the tape on the right side of the fabric with one end level with the edge. Lay the facing on top with right sides together, trapping the tape between. Stitch a seam 1.5cm (⅝in) from the edge, then neaten the raw edge on the opposite side of the facing (1). Press the facing on one back piece out flat and the other one under so that the seam with the tapes protruding sits on the edge. Tack the 2 sides together at the ends with the facings overlapped, so that the tapes can be tied (2). Make up the rest of the cushion, remove all the tacking, trim the seam allowance diagonally across the corners and turn the cover through.

BORDERS AND EDGINGS

Borders and edgings define the outline of a cushion, emphasizing its shape or framing a design. Choose a border or edging that complements the fabric and style of the cushion cover; for example, a piped edge is smart while a plain fringe is more informal. For the cushions in this book I have chosen simple edgings, because the emphasis is on the surface decoration, but you might prefer to complement the designs with less intricate covers but fancier edgings.

plain seamed edge

After the fastening has been completed, the cushion front is attached to the cushion back with a flat seam.

Place the front and back pieces together with right sides facing, matching the raw edges, then pin and tack them in position. Machine stitch the seam 1.5cm (⅝in) from the edge, securing the threads at both ends with a few reverse stitches. To create a neat corner, leave the needle in the fabric, lift the machine foot and rotate the fabric through 90 degrees, lower the foot and continue stitching. Trim the seam allowance diagonally across the corners, so that when the cover is turned through the corner can be pushed out to a neat point, and remove the tacking. If the fabric is likely to fray, finish the edges with pinking shears, oversewing or machine zigzag stitch (1).

To hand stitch a cushion cover, use backstitch to sew the seams and put in zips. Finish raw edges with oversewing (2) or blanket stitch (3).

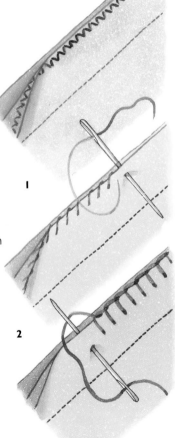

**1 Finishing edges with
zigzag stitch
2 Finishing edges with
oversewing
3 Finishing edges with
blanket stitch**

**1 Stitching the cushion front and back together
2 Working the stitching line to create the border**

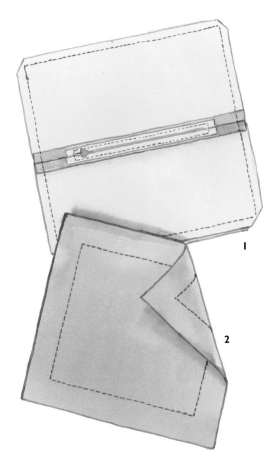

Oxford or single flange border

An Oxford or single flange border is a very neat and simple way to finish the edge of a cushion. The dimensions of the cover should be the same as those of the cushion pad, with an additional amount all round for the edging – usually about 3–5cm (1⅛–2in) plus 1.5cm (⅝in) seam allowance. Attach the cushion front to the back using a flat seam, then trim the seam allowance diagonally across the corners (1). Turn the cover through and roll the seam to the edge, tacking and then pressing it in place. Take care to push out the corners to a nice sharp point. Tack, then stitch a second line of straight or closely spaced zigzag stitching at the required distance from the edge to create the border (2). Remove the tacking.

piped edge

Piping is made by encasing a cord in a strip of fabric that has been cut diagonally to the grain of the fabric, which is called the bias. Bias binding and covered cord are available but in a limited range of colours, so getting a good match or finding the exact colour you want is easier if you make your own.

To make bias binding, fold a square of fabric diagonally to form a triangle: the folded edge will be the bias line. Using a ruler and tailor's chalk, mark a series of lines parallel to the bias line. The strips must be wide enough to cover the cord, with an additional 1.5cm (⅝in) allowance for the seam. Calculate how much piping is required, then cut and join enough bias strips to cover it. Bias strips must be joined together along the straight grain. Place the strips right sides together, with the cut ends matching, then pin and stitch, taking a 6mm (¼in) seam allowance. Press the seam open and trim off the points (1).

To cover the cord, place the cord on the wrong side of the bias strip and then fold the strip in half over the cord. Pin and stitch it in place as close to the cord as possible, using a piping or zipper foot attachment on the sewing machine (2).

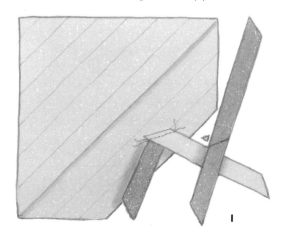

1 Joining both strips

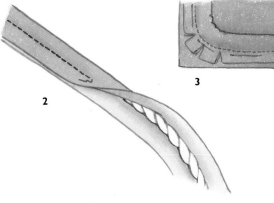

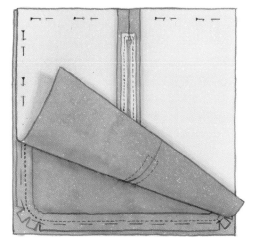

2 **Covering the cord**
3 **Tacking the cord to the cushion front**
4 **Stitching the cord ends together**
5 **Inserting the covered piping into the cushion seam**

To apply the piping to the cushion cover, tack the piping on the right side of the cushion front with the cord facing inwards, matching the raw edges of the piping and the fabric and clipping the corners of the piping to ease it around the cushion front (3). Start and stop tacking 5cm (2in) from the ends of the cord to make joining them easier. Cut the cord, allowing an extra 2cm (¾in) at each end. Unpick the cord stitching on the extra 2cm (¾in) and trim back the cord inside by about 2cm (¾in) so that the 2 ends of the cord can be butted up together. Stitch the cord ends together and overlap the excess covering fabric, turning under 1cm (⅜in) on the top layer to cover the raw edges (4). Pin and join up the gap in the tacking.

Place the cushion back piece of the cover on top with the right side down, so that the piping is sandwiched between the cushion back and front. Pin, tack and machine stitch the seam around the cushion cover as close to the piping as possible (5). Remove the tacking. When the cover is turned through, the piping should sit neatly on the line of the seam.

fringes

A fringe is a loosely hanging decorative trim that adds texture to a cushion. The strands hanging down can be plain or twisted, knotted or beaded, and may incorporate tassels or pompons. Flanged fringes are applied in much the same way as piping,

with the flange being included in the seam. With the right sides of the cushion front and back facing each other, sandwich the fringe between them with the decorative edge pointing inwards and the flange parallel with the edge of the fabric. Then stitch the seam through all 3 layers. How much of the heading is included in the seam depends on how fancy it is and how much is required to show. Fringes can also be hand stitched to the completed cover, over the seamline.

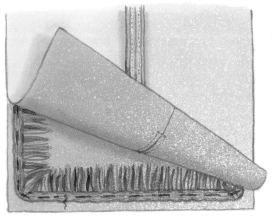

Inserting a fringe into the cushion seam

**Inserting a ruffle into
the cushion seam**

ruffles

A ruffle is a gathered strip of fabric, usually light in weight, which gives a soft edge to the cushion. The strip of fabric for the ruffle should be twice the length of the edge to which it is to be applied. Gather it with 2 rows of running stitch pulled up to half the length, then apply it to the cushion in the same way as a fringe. If the ruffle goes around all 4 sides of the cushion, seam the 2 ends together neatly. If it is on 2 opposite sides of the cushion only, neaten both ends and pin the fullness out of the path of the adjacent seams before stitching.

tassels

Tassels are decorative bunches of yarn. They can be purchased in a limited range of colours but are very easy to make yourself, opening up a wide choice of yarns and colours.

Cut 2 rectangular pieces of card of the same size. The depth of the rectangle determines the finished length of the tassel. Place the 2 pieces of card together and wrap the yarn around them. With the yarn still on the card, insert a length of the same yarn between the 2 pieces of card and under the wrapped yarn (1). Tie this tightly to hold the tassel together, but do not trim the ends of the knotted yarn as they can be used to attach the tassel. Cut through the wrapped yarn at the other side of the card, slipping the scissors between the 2 layers of card, which can then be removed. Bind the tassel 1.25cm (½in) from the top of the uncut end, oversewing the binding thread at the start and finish, then thread the end back into the tassel top for a neat finish (2).

**1 Inserting a length of
yarn between the
pieces of card
2 Binding the tassel**

MAKING A CIRCULAR CUSHION

First make a paper pattern of the required size. Tie a pencil to one end of a length of string and press a drawing pin through the other end: the distance between pencil and drawing pin should be equal to the radius of the finished cushion plus 1.5cm (⅝in) seam allowance. Fold a large sheet of paper into quarters, lay it on an old board and press the drawing pin in at the corner where all the folds meet. With the string taut and the pencil vertical, draw an arc to mark a quarter circle on the paper (1). Cut out the shape through all the layers of paper and open it out to form the full circle.

Pin the paper pattern to the embroidered cushion front and trim the fabric into a circle. To make a pattern for the 2 back pieces, fold the

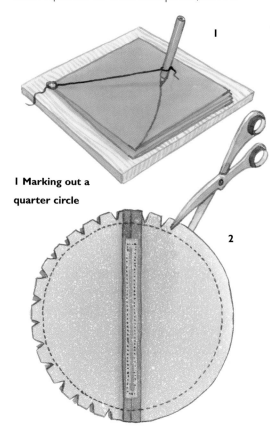

**1 Marking out a
quarter circle**

2 Cutting notches in the seam allowance

circular pattern in half and add 1.5cm (⅝in) seam allowance along the straight side. Cut V-shaped notches in the seam allowance around the circumference of the fabric, as the seam is curved (2). Finish the cushion with the edge and fastening of your choice.

MAKING A BOLSTER CUSHION

You will need a piece of fabric of the required size plus 1.5cm (⅝n) seam allowance all round, plus 2 strips for the ends. These should be the same width as the main piece and deep enough to cover the end of the cushion plus 5cm (2in). Fold the main piece of fabric and the 2 end strips in half with right sides facing and stitch a seam along each to form 3 tubes. When stitching the seam on the main piece, leave a gap for the zip 1cm (⅜in) longer than the length covered by the zip teeth, including the top and bottom stops (1). Press the seams open and insert the zip into the main tube (see page 102). Stitch the piping around the ends of the main tube, then attach the smaller tubes, right sides facing, to the ends with the piping trapped in between (2). Turn right sides out and gather the end pieces 3.5 cm (1⅜in) from the edge, tucking the extra fabric inside (3). Secure the gathering threads and finish the ends of the bolster with buttons.

PADS AND FILLINGS

Cushion pads are available in standard sizes with feather or man-made fillings inside a polyester/cotton cover. You may need to make your own pad if the cushion is a non-standard size or you are on a tight budget. Use a strong, hardwearing fabric such as ticking or calico to cover the filling, so that the decorative cover can be removed and washed.

Down or down-and-feather mix both make a very comfortable cushion that will retain its shape, but they are quite expensive and some people are allergic to them. It is particularly important to use a

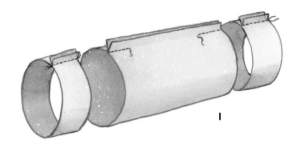

closely woven fabric to cover these pads to prevent the sharp ends of the feathers poking through. A fleecy polyester filling is a good choice as it is relatively inexpensive, comfortable and retains its shape reasonably well. I would not recommend latex or foam chips, as they are lumpy and do not hold their shape.

Square and rectangular pads are made using the slipstitched opening technique (see page 102). To make a firm cushion, the pad can be slightly bigger than the cushion cover. Always be generous with the stuffing, as it will lose some of its bulk in use. To make an inner for a bolster, sew a piece of fabric of the same dimensions as the outer cushion into a tube, leaving a gap in the seam. Stitch on circular ends, notch the seam allowances and then turn right side out. A bolster should be very firm so pack it well with stuffing before slipstitching the seam closed.

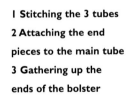

**1 Stitching the 3 tubes
2 Attaching the end
pieces to the main tube
3 Gathering up the
ends of the bolster**

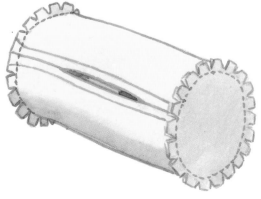

**Notch the seam
allowances when
making a bolster inner**

index

Projects are
shown in *italic*

A

ammonites 18
anemones 58–61
appliqué
   Fossil Appliqué 18–21
   Heartsease 82–85

B

backstitch 101
blinds, *Clover* 95
blockweave fabrics 96
bolsters 109
   Chilli Peppers 42–44
border designs
   Feathers 88–90
   Patchwork Hellebore
     31
   Peacock and Jewel 48
borders 105–108
buttons 104
   Citrus 66–69

C

calming rooms 8–11
charts, reading 99
Chilli Peppers 42–45
circular cushions
   108–109
Citrus 66–69
Clover 92–95
colours
   bright 54–57
   natural 8–11
   pale 74–77

   rich 32–35
corner designs,
   Modesty 80
covered boxes, *Citrus* 69
cross stitch 100–101
curtains, *Heartsease* 85
cushions
circular 108–109
   Citrus 66–69
   Clover 92–94
   Feathers 86–89
   Flower Power 58–60
   Fossil Appliqué 18–20
   Gladiolus 50–52
   Heartsease 82–84
   Ivy Spiral 12–15
   making up 101
   Modesty 78–81
   Organza Leaf 36–39
   Patchwork Hellebore
     28–30
   Peacock and Jewel
     46–48
   Sea Shells 22–25
   Trailing Nasturtiums
     70–73
   Tropical Knit 62–65

D

delphiniums 61
dyeing fabrics 96–97

E

equipment 96–98
evenweave fabrics 96

F

fabrics
   blockweave 96
   dyeing 96–97
   evenweave 96
   measuring 101
   preparation 98–99
   washing 101
fastenings 102–105
Feathers 86–91
feathers 46–49, 86–91
Flower Power 58–61
Fossil Appliqué 18–21
fringes 107

G

Gladiolus 50–53

H

Heartsease 82–85
helianthus 58–61
hellebores 28–31
hoops 99

I

irises 58–61
Ivy Spiral 12–17

J

jewels 46–49

K

knitting 62–65

L

lampshades, *Fossil*
   Appliqué 21

Editorial Manager: **Jane Birch**
Senior Designer: **Claire Harvey**
Designer: **Lisa Tai**
Photographer: **Sandra Lane**
Illustrator: **Kate Simunek**
Picture Researcher: **Jennifer Veall**
Production Controller: **Jo Sim**

Author's Acknowledgements

I would like to thank **Patricia** and **Catherine Birkett** and **Joan Evans** for their invaluable help in embroidering the designs for the book.

My thanks also to **Coats Crafts UK,** for supplying all the embroidery threads and basic embroidery fabrics (tel. 01325 365 857 for stockists). Many thanks to **Fabric Flair**, for their dyed evenweave fabrics (tel. 01985 846400 for stockists), and to **J.A.B. Anstoetz** for their beautiful velvet and silk furnishing fabrics (tel. 020 7349 9323 for stockists). Thanks also to **Dylon International Ltd** for their advice on dyeing embroidery fabrics (tel. 020 8663 4296 for stockists), and to **W. Rouleaux**, for their trimmings (tel. 020 7730 3125).

Photographic Acknowledgements
(in Source Order)

Crown 76 Bottom Left
Flowers & Foliage/Ashton 92 Top
Octopus Publishing Group Ltd. 4 Bottom Right, 5 Bottom Right, 12 Bottom, 28, 36 Top, 46 Top, 55 Top Left, 57 Bottom, 62 Bottom, 70, 82 Bottom/**Bill Reavell** 55 Bottom Centre/David Loftus 4 Bottom Left, 5 Bottom Left, 10, 22 Top, 26 Bottom, 55 Bottom Left, 57 Top, 58 Top, 58 Bottom, 62 Top, 66 Top, 66 Bottom, 76 Bottom Right/**David Parmitter** 56 Bottom Right/**Debi Treloar** 9 Bottom Left/**Di Lewis** 75 Top Right, 77/**Ian Wallace** 9 Top Right/**Jacqui Wornell** 75 Bottom Right/**Jean Cazals** 56-57 Top/**Linda Burgess** 11 Bottom Right/**London Back & White** 48 Top Right 16, 21 Top, 25 Top, 30 Top, 38 Top Right, 44 Bottom, 52 right, 61 Top Left, 65 Top Left, 69 Top, 72 Top Right, 80 Top Right, 84 Top Right, 89 Top Right, 94 Bottom/**Mark Winwood** 7 Bottom Left, 7 Bottom Right, 11 Bottom Left, 12 Top, 26 Top, 34 Top, 40, 46 Bottom, 50, 51, 86, 89 Bottom Left, 92 Bottom/Mel Yates 11 Bottom Centre/**Michael Boys** 82 Top/**Peter Myers** 55 Top Right/**Polly Wreford** 6 Top Centre, 9 Centre Left, 9 Bottom Right, 11 Top Right, 22 Bottom, 33 Top Left, 33 Top Right, 33 Bottom Right, 35, 56 Bottom Left, 75 Bottom Centre/**Sandra Lane** 1, 2-3, 4 Top Left, 4 Top Right, 5 Top Left, 6 Top Left, 6 Top Right, 6 Bottom, 7 Top Right, 7 Bottom Centre, 8 Top Left, 8 Top Centre, 8 Top Right, 13, 17, 18-19, 21 Bottom, 23, 27, 29, 31 Bottom Right, 32 Top Left, 32 Top Centre, 32 Top Right, 37, 41, 42, 43, 45 right, 47, 48 Bottom Left, 52, 54 Top Left, 54 Top Centre, 54 Top Right, 59, 61 right, 63, 65 Bottom Right, 66-67, 69 Bottom, 71, 72 Bottom Left, 74 Top Left, 74 Top Centre, 74 Top Right, 79, 80 Bottom Left, 83, 85, 87, 91, 93, 95/**Simon Smith** 55 Centre Right, 76 Top Left/Tom Mannion 34 Bottom/**Bill Patten** 78
Next 36 Bottom
Osborne & Little plc 18 left, 75 Top Left